Blackbird—a Memoir

The Story of a Woman that Submitted to Marcial Maciel,
Became Free, and Found Happiness Again

Elena Sada

Dedication

To all of the men and women who have been hurt by deceit, I wish to offer a vision of optimism and a touch of humor.

To all of the children—for their minds and consciences are most vulnerable to evil deceit and manipulation—and to their parents, that they will have the wisdom to protect them from manipulation. May all be safeguarded from surrendering their conscience to another human being.

Acknowledgements

I'd like to thank my group of childhood friends—or as we affectionately call it, "tunnel friends," since our friendship connects us through time and space—for they asked me to write this book hoping it will help others.

A very special thanks to my editor and friend, Trish Bailey, for her brilliant talent, support, and empathy; to photographer, Kameron Kicklighter, for representing the essence of my story in the book cover; and to writers and friends Lorea Canales and Roberta Garza, as well as, Elena Barrero—for they encouraged me to write without losing sight of my own values and voice.

I am grateful to my therapists, Vickie Ehrilich and Mari DeRoche: their timely counseling allowed me to reflect on *my process* and embrace vulnerability.

I specially thank all Regnum Christi members—those who exited, and those who remain—for their examples inspired and motivated me to write every single word in this book.

I can't thank my children enough, for simply "being;" I am grateful that I can love them with all my heart, and that my desire to protect them extends to all children.

I thank my mother for showing me how to live life passionately, and for sharing with me her love for writing; and my father, for teaching me to believe in people's goodness, and to always do what I think is right. I'd like to thank my siblings for supporting me with kindness and patience, and for reading my manuscript and offering helpful recommendations.

Very especially, I thank my companion and partner, *Edward*—who has been instrumental in my healing process. His inspiration and encouragement made this book possible.

"I leave this life with no regrets. It was a wonderful life—full and complete with the great loves and great endeavors that make it worth living. I am sad to leave, but I leave with the knowledge that I lived the life that I intended."

    Charles Krauthammer, June 8, 2018
    —two weeks before his death

Table of Contents

Introduction   9

Prologue   11

PART I
First Year After RC   13

Chapter 1 "That Day"   15
Chapter 2 My First Day "Out"   21
Chapter 3 Abstinence   29
Chapter 4 Shame   37
Chapter 5 Team Balance   45
Chapter 6 Destiny   51
Chapter 7 An Angel   55
Chapter 8 Trapped   63
Chapter 9 Daring   69
Chapter 10 Friends   81
Chapter 11 Identity   91

PART II
Vindicating—Yet Horrific—Truth   95

Chapter 12 Maciel   97
Chapter 13 First Youth and Family Encounter   105
Chapter 14 Dealing With the News   107
Chapter 15 The Hullaballoo   115
Chapter 16 A Cult   123
Chapter 17 Everyone Deserves a Second Chance   127

PART III
Living the Life I Intend to Live   135

Chapter 18 Patrimony   137
Chapter 19 Teacher   143
Chapter 20 Advocate   149
Chapter 21 Mother   157
Chapter 22 Ongoing Beginnings   161
Chapter 23 Death   165
Chapter 24 I Can Cook   167
Chapter 25 The Value of Patience   173
Chapter 26 Words Are Not Just Words   179
Chapter 27 Next Step in Our Relationship   185
Chapter 28 Decluttering   191
Chapter 29 Cross While the Tide Is Low   197
Chapter 30 A Car-Wash Moment   201
Chapter 31 Broken   205

Epilogue   209

Author's Note   211

Vignettes from Research and the Imagination   213

Maciel's Punishment   215
Maciel and a Second Woman   221
Maciel and a Third Woman   225
First Daughter   229
From the Mouth of Babes, Drunks, and Drug Addict   233

Introduction

For 18 years, I was a member of the Catholic movement, Regnum Christi, which was associated with a religious order called the Legion of Christ. Many considered this religious infrastructure to be a cult. What I have learned since I left the movement, in November of 2001, moved me to write this book. It is only fair to begin by saying that currently, since the departure of many of us, and some horrific information released by media, both the order and the movement are in the process of making changes.

Father Marcial Maciel, LC was a Mexican priest of Spanish and French descent who founded the order of priests, the Legion of Christ in the 1940s—and later, Regnum Christi—in Mexico, Spain, Italy, and Ireland. Sixty years later, after decades of accusations of numerous crimes, Pope Benedict XVI requested Maciel to retire and "live a life of penance and prayer." He died two years later and was never condemned in civil court, despite evidence of his theft and serial pedophile activity.

While the Vatican and dioceses study ways to stop the flash flood of sexual abuse committed by Catholic priests worldwide, the Catholic laity—unintentionally—continue to facilitate their criminal behavior. I am not suggesting that the clergy, the offenders, are innocent; I am simply establishing a fatal connection between the way the many laity treat priests and their crimes. As long as the laity treat priests like superhumans, some of them will take on the role of a superior caste, and be more tempted to live above the civil order. We are the enablers of their narcissistic fictional world where they are in charge of the rules, and not subjects under them.

My story reflects the unique way in which I lived and remember the events. I created the dialogues from memory. Some names, locations, and other identifying characteristics have been changed to protect individuals' privacy. All of the short dreams that I recount, I did actually dream. I include them because they spoke to me at the time and helped me discern my way.

Cults are not something from the past. Currently, hundreds of children and youth are drawn into cults and are subjects of emotional and/or physical abuse.

Elena Sada
August 18, 2018, Blue Ridge Mountains, North Carolina

Prologue

I was born in Monterrey's rocky mountains, in the north of Mexico, but I could be from anywhere. In fact, I became from nowhere.

I am the great granddaughter of the co-founder of Cuauhtemoc Brewery, home of the Dos XX, Tecate, Sol, and Bohemia beers. I am the daughter of the co-founder of Pronatura, one of the most active conservation and ecological groups in Latin America. I was admitted into Georgetown University's School of Foreign Service, in Washington, D.C., when I was 16. This was to no one's surprise, after all, both my father and grandfather attended MIT (the Massachusetts Institute of Technology) in Boston, and were successful CEOs of multinational companies. My family was friends with some of the wealthiest men and women in Latin America and the USA... but then, so was Marcial Maciel, a priest and the founder of the group I joined when I was barely 19.

This is my story. It tells the way I learned to hide, to cry, survive, and then laugh again... and laugh some more, since I learned to see life with a humor that is not sarcasm, but hope... and because I learned to *live* and never again just *survive*.

This is what happened on that day not long after the 9/11 attacks on the World Trade Center and the Pentagon, not long after the fall of the Berlin Wall and the end of the Soviet Union. Not even that long after the ending of South Africa's apartheid system. The world was faced with a choice between life and death, and it chose to live... hurting, but alive... and so did I on that day. It was the day I "escaped" from the convent—or almost convent, or more than a convent—at 37 years of age.

12

Part I

First Year After RC

14

Chapter 1

THAT DAY

I looked at my watch; I had grabbed it after my last trip to the bathroom at 4:07 a.m. It was 5:25 a.m. I had lived that moment so many times in my head. It was finally there. Something told me that if I didn't do it then, it would never happen… and I would choose a slow death. I needed to escape. Catching the wave of the adrenaline high before exhaustion took over, as I knew it eventually would, I slid my legs to the side of the bed and held my breath. Slowly, I raised my head over the pillow. I don't know why I scanned the room, why I expected it to be different; it had been the same since the Legion of Christ bought the house. The Legion, directed by Father Marcial Maciel—a thief, pedophile—was the order that managed and supervised Regnum Christi, the Catholic organization to which I had belonged for almost 20 years. Father Maciel had founded first the priestly branch and then Regnum Christi, with its female consecrated branch. These were women who would make promises to live in total poverty, obedience and chastity, and who lived in communities under the "statutes" dictated by Maciel.

I needed to make it to the downstairs bathroom with my shoes and my dress. The monologue was exhausting me already. Why did I always have to talk myself so much into doing things? I looked at the end of the bed… my dress was still there. I felt pain in my chest when I realized I didn't know where my passport was or who had it. I closed my eyes and rested my head on the pillow again. I told myself I would have to do without it for a few days, maybe forever—I could surely get a new one, couldn't I? I would explain it had been stolen; in a way, it was true. In Regnum Christi, I had learned that if you only mention the one part of the lie that is true, then you are not really lying.

As carefully as possible, I slowly placed both feet on the wooden floor, which—like the air—was cold. I decided not to wear slippers; they could be noisy. The slippers would be left behind together with everything that had not been mine, but had been for my use: a few dresses, a brush, and a couple of pantyhose. Since I lived in poverty, I only had a few things on hand. I looked at the slippers on the floor, next to the bed. They would be left behind "out of place"… probably the only item out of place in the room, or in the entire house. The slippers would be my legacy: "A woman left the movement after 18 years, a woman who was supposed to be a model to follow, a beacon of light, a national vocational director… that woman once laid on the bed where her slippers remain." Then, the director of the center—the woman designated by Maciel to ensure that the "statutes" were meticulously followed—would notice I was gone and, after informing the Legionary priest in charge of the community, would discreetly gather everything I left behind… "Who had she been?" she would later ask.

Very slowly, I pushed myself up and out of the bed. My two-piece pajamas sagged on my body like the clock in Dalí's painting. Two-piece pajamas—not gowns—are the only type we were allowed to wear… and though I never asked why, it was understood that it was a measure taken so our legs wouldn't be accidentally exposed during the night. I needed to get out and catch the train to D.C before everyone would awake. I took the dress, and with my eyes on the women sleeping, I quietly walked towards the bedroom door.

As I peeked outside into the hall, I grabbed my shoes…a pair of brown dull loafers neatly placed outside of the bedroom together with my roommates' shoes. The hallway seemed to be empty. I couldn't be sure; it was completely dark. I passed by a room with three beds with a woman sleeping on each. "They can't wake up. If I do leave, no one should know." Heather was sleeping on one of the beds. I could clearly hear her inhale and exhale; she was a heavy sleeper. Ana, on the bed at the opposite side, was cuddling her blanket under her chin. I didn't know who the woman in the middle was… there were several of us in that house. Because of her position, I couldn't help but think Ana still missed a childhood teddy bear; or it could also be that the deprivation of affection we experienced surfaced from her unconsciousness during the night, and she needed to hug her blanket. On the other hand, she was probably also feeling, like I did, the fall cold breeze from the Potomac River that, together with the light of a shy moon, found its way into the room through an open window.

A flickering light at the bottom of the central stairs had found its intermittent way up to the second floor, and was shining on some objects. There was not enough light to account for everything in the hallway but enough to find my way down: past the donated grandfather's clock, a small table outside of the director's room… and shoes… an army of pairs of shoes lined outside of each of the five bedrooms on the second floor. We would place them there so they could vent overnight and so their smell wouldn't settle in the bedrooms forever. Poor shoes… the only time in the entire day when they were not carrying us around was during the seven hours we slept—eight hours if you counted the half an hour we had to get ready for bed at night, and in the morning. As I walked towards the stairs, I felt like everything was watching my every move: the shoes were jealous, the clock stared with an open mouth, the table took note so as to include it with the other notes resting on it and be ready to retell the story of my departure to the director. Even the objects below the stairs—a lazy deemed lamp and a bored armchair… because no one would ever sit on it—judged me. Were they accusing me for fleeing? How can objects with no eyes stare at you? I stopped making eye contact just in case, and continued to walk towards the stairs. *You can judge me, but you cannot stop me.* However, as I placed a foot on the first step, I heard the loudest cracking cry a floorboard has ever made. How can the house have learned to telltale? *Please. Have mercy.* Could my plea make the ancient colonial house change her mind? I placed my other foot on the second step… no more squeaking. *Thank you, God—and the house… you might still have a heart after all.* I continued my descent with my head turned back and my eyes fixed on the top of the stairs, hoping for no one to wake up, waiting for someone to wake up.

As I went down I saw, through the corner of my eye, a picture that had always been there: one where Father Maciel holds the Eucharist during the consecration in Mass. His priestly ornaments are white and the background is gold. Everything about the picture is mystical. Father Maciel's expression seemed in trance. But as I continued my descent, his eyes warned: "Elena, when a woman closes the door to her religious or consecrated vocation, she will carry on her shoulders the weight of the sins of the souls she was destined to save, but omitted to do so… because she was weak and selfish." The word *selfish* echoed and my eyes squinted as if the gesture could prevent it from repeating inside my head. Maciel's voice got louder with every step. I ignored it. My body was raggedy and bloody after the mortal fight I endured in my dream while sleeping, but my voice was still strong: *I am sorry, Father Maciel. Tonight I choose to live. Your warning—threat—will not stop me this time.*

I reached the bottom of the stairs and walked at a steady pace to the bathroom next to the main door. I had approximately 10 minutes before the alarm clock would release those annoying pip-pip-pips in the director's room, followed by the routine morning sounds: sliding slippers under tired feet moving quickly to each room. "Christ our King!" the director would cry, and our drowsy voices coming from inside of the rooms would reply, "Your Kingdom Come!" The noises would then be muffled by other similar noises: showers, doors, and more slippers. We were not allowed to be barefoot in the house. We were not allowed to talk either. Instead, we were supposed to recite in our head Psalm 51, The Miserere —"Have mercy on us, oh God; wash me from my wickedness and cleanse me from my sins. Surely I was sinful at birth, sinful from the time my mother conceived me."

I reached the bathroom by the main door, the one reserved for visitors, and quietly closed the door behind me. I carefully placed the shoes on the floor and the dress by the sink. I rubbed my hands instinctively—they were shaking. I was unsure if I could use the toilet without waking someone up. Of course, I used it; people have needs in the middle of the night… no one can control that, can they? They had control over everything else. I knew I couldn't flush. On any other day, under different circumstances, I would feel bad… my conscience would protest and call me selfish for not leaving the toilet ready for others to use… but not on "that day."

I lifted my pajama top and took it off, followed by my bottoms. Had it not been for the need to hurry, I would have stayed there, looking at my naked body in the mirror. Unlike the other bathrooms in the house, the visitor's bathroom downstairs had a large mirror over the sink; I had never been naked there. Besides, due to the way the shower turns were scheduled, we had only three minutes of daily bathroom use in the mornings. We hardly had time to account for all body parts, let alone look at each of them. I stared at myself for several more seconds: from my noticeable cheekbones, elongated neck, my smaller than ever, rounded, and still young breasts over a symmetrical rack of ribs, my hipbones and legs. I could trace with perfection my body's skeleton. I was a disgusting five feet eight inches, 100 pounds even—I weighed 30 pounds less than when I entered, and I was average and athletic then. When had I starved myself? I had become well aware of my affective starvation throughout the years, but not of my physical starvation. Maybe it was a way to avoid feeling the inner starvation… like when you get a vaccine shot and, to distract the mind from that pain, you sink a nail into a finger, making it hurt.

I slipped the dress over my head and my hips. Then I quickly put my shoes on. I felt naked under the dress—for the first time since age 18, I could feel my bare breasts, thighs, and knees under the dress… no rule-abiding slip or nylons on "that day."

As I opened the bathroom door and gazed outside carefully, I turned to the living room one last time. The Potomac Center, in Maryland, was not "my center"—as we would call our homes or the houses where we had been assigned to live. I was a mere visitor, asked to be there for a few weeks to undergo a psychological "consultation." And since the psychiatrist had already offered her prognosis and prescribed an antidepressant, I was supposed to fly back to "my center" in California. My case was just a typical case of depression; the medication would "do the trick." In California, I would resume my duties as a teacher, as the Center's supervisor, and as vocational director for North America, Australia, and New Zealand. As I looked at the living room, I thought I would definitely not miss the house or anything in it. My throat tightened. I would miss Anna and Mary... and everyone with whom I had worked and had left behind around the country every time I was transferred to a new center.

When I was about to turn towards the main door, I heard a noise coming from an upstairs bedroom. A gasp escaped my mouth before I quickly covered it with a hand. For lack of a better place, I held my pajamas under my arm and hurriedly took a couple of long strides towards the main door, and ignoring the tap-tap sound of my shoes, I stepped into the breezy remains of the night. I thought I heard my name at a distance, but since I could not trust the voice, I did not turn back. I knew that if I walked fast enough, I could make it to the train station before dawn. I touched the pocket on my chest. The Metro card was still there.

Chapter 2

MY FIRST DAY "OUT"

It was the fall of 2001, several weeks after the 9/11 attacks on the World Trade Center and the Pentagon. The tragedy of four planes… carrying our sons, mothers, brothers, sisters and friends… crashing on our people and our land—used as missiles—had shaken everyone to the core. I was in Arlington, Virginia on that day and had seen the Pentagon in flames. The brain that directs our nation's defense was pierce by a bullet carrying our own blood. No doubt the attack extracted from our land some of the most genuine feelings of patriotism my generation has ever seen. On the crisp morning I escaped, November 1st, the Day of All Saints, I decided to come out from my grave and live… as much as the saints in heaven lived, as much as the patriotism of our country had come alive.

I took the Metro from Potomac towards Washington D.C at 6:30 a.m. My escape was triggered by a scream in the middle of the night… and though there might have been other screams in the house that night, I was certain it had been my own shout that woke me up and made me leave. As I sat on the train, its monotonous rocking demanded an explanation. And so I began to replay my night: It was a dream… one of those very real dreams. *I am in Rome, at Regnum Christi's Center and College. I walk to the orchard on the top of the hill. I leave behind the huge midrise red brick building with a cross on the top and multiple wings, used as dormitories and classrooms. The gardens are beautifully kept, interrupted only by parking spaces and two basketball courts. As I approach the plot where carrots and other vegetables were planted, I lean down to examine them. I hear the commotion: two ferocious dogs growling under a fig tree. On one of its branches, a scared kitten tries to stay out of reach; her four legs cling to the branch in an embrace. Her claws have a weak grip on its thin bark. The dogs jump against the fragile tree trunk. With every jump, the kitten loses balance and is close to falling. Her hair is brown and her eyes are honey. Please little kitten... please stay put... hold on, I'm almost there. I keep trying to make my heavy legs move faster... with no luck. One of the dogs jumps again and places his front legs forcefully against the fig tree's trunk. The little feline loses balance miserably and hopelessly. I shut my eyes. What follows is grotesque and I brace myself once again for the horror. The dog grabs her instantly between its teeth and begins to shake her faintish body relentlessly. Blood splatters right and left. I moan. In the dream, I screamed.*

Tears rolled down my cheeks again. When I opened my eyes, I realized there were two men and a woman in the train car... business commuters. I scanned their faces quickly. They were looking at me. I wiped my tears. No need to worry them.

I closed my eyes again. *Was that it? Was it the end for the cat? I reach the bloody scene. The dog is still pressing her fully in its jaw and continues to agitate her small furry body, which is by now almost dead and soaking in blood. God! Part of me wants to let her die... a charitable choice... a quick escape from suffering. The other part wants to unpin her from the dog's fangs. I second-guess myself... an extremely familiar habit. Even if I unpin her, she will probably die.*

My tears reached my neck... I even felt them on my chest. The train car kept rocking me... *how generous.* I become aware that it stopped and then moved again. My lips said the words: "I choose to live... hurting but alive." I tasted the saltiness of the tears and I wet my lips with my tongue. The image came back: a bloody lifeless cat... I am scarred and hurting, but alive. I know I am alive because I feel the pain and the wetness on my chest, the saltiness of my tears... as well as the sweet rocking of the train.

The daily commuters were still staring at me and a middle aged woman—wearing an elegant suit—was sitting by my side. She gently placed her hand over mine. "Is there anything I can do for you?" She gave me a timid smile. Seven weeks back, commuters on that same train lost their lives in the Pentagon, so a crying passenger was not an unusual sight. I managed to return the smile. "Thank you. I am alive." *I think I meant to say, "I am OK."* She seemed confused for an instant only, and then a grin appeared on her face. Maybe because, somehow, there is an understanding between us… Maybe we all experience—at least once in our life—that hopelessness and hope co-exist, since we must be alive to feel anything, including hopelessness… and if we are alive, then there is hope.

I closed my eyes again and placed myself at the orchard. *With both arms and all the strength of my soul, I force open the dog's red snout. The kitten's body, raw and shapeless, falls to the ground. I reach out to grab and hold her against my chest as carefully and as quickly as I can.* The cat can live or die and it will be determined by my choice. If she lives, she will live wounded... she will require healing; and maybe she will never completely heal. The dog's attack will always be part of her past life. But that is the only option, the option I chose when I got out of bed and out of the house that morning. The other option—that of a slow death caused by the asphyxiation of my conscience and my emotions—is not an alternative for someone who wants a second chance. Living with a hurt is better than vanishing. Loving with a hurt is better than pinning your heart between the tusks of disheartening confusion and guilt.

I got off the train at Crystal City, Virginia, right outside of downtown D.C. My friend Emma lived nearby… a friendship I almost lost because we were not allowed to have "friends" in Regnum Christi. Emma, a mother of four, was already up when I called. We spoke and made a plan.

Then, the tough call "home" to my family, was next on the list.

"You don't have to explain anything, sweetie," I heard my dad say when he picked up the phone. I had started to cry as soon as I heard his voice. And since I continued crying, he added: "Why don't you come home? Where are you?"

I knew that the most rational thing to do was to "come home," but I couldn't. I wasn't ready for all the questions that would inevitably follow my departure. I was physically and emotionally exhausted. How could I tell everyone I had left because I had reached a level of confusion that was making me physically ill? How could Elena Sada, a woman who had always preached that in moments of emotional darkness is better to "remain still," admit that she had fled in a moment of confusion? Was the enlightenment from a dream enough to justify my departure? I knew it was for me, but I couldn't explain it… at least, not yet.

My father sent me a copy of my birth certificate, which—of course—he had kept in case of "an emergency." And then I did something Regnum Christi had trained me to do well: I asked him for money. He agreed to help me financially for six months. "After that," he said, "either you come home or you will need to support yourself." His voice was measured, calm, and affectionate… but, as always, he was also firm. He had asked me if I wanted to speak to my mother. I simply suggested to him to let her know I was taking time "off"… and promised to write to them soon. Back then my mother was Maciel's supporter… like many other wonderful people, in Monterrey, were. I didn't think I could explain to her why I left.

After what I had done—leave Regnum Christi without telling Maciel—giving my dad the news had not been hard at all. I left without Maciel's blessing. He was God's representative on earth and everyone who leaves needed his blessing. I did not write to him or call him; maybe because I knew Maciel wouldn't grant the permission without making me feel guilty and ashamed. Or maybe I didn't ask him because

I was just too exhausted to even think, or feel, or care. I just needed to remain alive.

Later that day, despite Emma's plea to stay in her house, I found myself taking the train back to Potomac. I couldn't bear the thought of leaving without saying goodbye to some of the woman in the center. My departure that afternoon was not as dramatic but it was very sad. Only a few of the women found out because I arrived and left during community prayers.

That night, I settled in a loft Emma and I managed to rent on a month-to-month basis. My father agreed to pay and Emma's husband agreed to be my guarantor. Until this day, we joke about how I didn't pay my rent and he will probably receive the bill for the few months I was there, plus more than 15 years of interest. After Emma and I hugged and shared unspoken words, I walked into the empty loft, lay down on a borrowed bed, ate a banana, and slept. For a few days I slept with a peace I had forgotten could exist.

When I eventually found the strength to come out of the loft, it seemed like my years in Regnum Christi had been a very complex dream. I wanted to contact some people with whom I had worked during that time. A director in RC had already reached out to me, through Emma, to relay the message: "Please don't stir up the hornet's nest." My departure, nevertheless, had done more than that. After all, besides sharing the responsibility of establishing schools and other works, I had been the territorial vocational director for almost 10 years. I had traveled to 48 states, Canada, New Zealand, and Australia to meet families and women who had shown interest in joining RC.

After my departure, when former RC colleagues asked where I was, the answer usually was "Oh, she is probably traveling around like always." When it became obvious that I no longer had "a place" in one of RC's communities, other explanations were given; the most common was: "She got sick and left." Illness in RC meant incapacity to be productive and, therefore, those who could afford it preferred to leave—many times they were encouraged to leave. Maciel's choice of noun to label those who stayed in RC but did not work to make it grow was "parasites." Other times, it was said I left because I had not been given the ultimate leadership in the territory. In fact, a few weeks before my departure, another "more loyal" woman arrived from Italy to take over some of my work. The ultimate leadership for a woman in RC meant assisting the Territorial Director, a Legionary priest. I had gotten in trouble many times for insinuating that the Territorial Director had made a mistake. In RC, that meant breaking a solemn vow to never criticize a superior. So I was verbally scolded and punished. The punishment implied losing responsibilities, or being excluded from meetings reserved for "loyal leadership." It hurt… Since then, I have learned that worse things happen in the secular workplace when a boss can abuse their power. But since a workplace is not meant to replace your family, like RC did at such a young age, isolation in RC was excruciating painful.

Three months after I left, I landed a temporary internship at the United Nations in Manhattan. And, once there, it took me a week to find a studio I could afford—much smaller than the loft I had rented in Crystal City, Arlington. In addition to Emma's airbed, I had purchased some furniture and acquired a radio someone left next to the floor's garbage container in the back of my building. So as I used to do before I joined RC, I started to constantly dance by myself, in my loft. But this time, I danced to melodies I didn't know. I never caught up with the two decades of music I missed—the 80s and 90s. The music and the dancing, however, served as therapy to rewire my brain and produce dopamine—the happy hormone.

I had to catch up with much more than music and movies. I did not know how to behave with men, let alone be able to read their intentions and suggestions.

A man I will call Victor was my boss during a temporary internship and potential job in a Manhattan government office. I lasted three weeks there. The day I resigned, I was with Victor in his small office: a modern and bright room on the 16th floor of one of the city's skyscrapers. After writing some notes on a task he assigned me, I got up, and turning my back to him for only an instant while I gathered my bag and papers, I felt him... I felt his hands. He approached me from behind. I remained tense. I was hopelessly trapped between the sofa and Victor's body. Never in my naive mind had I considered this man capable of doing such a thing. He was married. Though I was shocked, I still had the wits to ask myself if my knee-length skirt—much shorter than what I used to wear in the movement—had been responsible for the "misunderstanding." Maybe at the workplace women were supposed to wear their blouses tucked into their skirt, I thought, as I felt his hands over my skin. *What did I do wrong?*

"No one will come in, if that's what worries you," he whispered over my shoulder, gluing his eyes on my lips and, surely, sensing the stiffness in my body. "I doubt I misread your attentions," he continued, almost out of breath. His hands were still moving under my blouse and he had managed to place his lips near mine. I fought the fear that my knees would give in. I even attempted to explain to him that I was simply fulfilling my duty, and had only been friendly.

It is true, I am generally cheerful, but I always considered myself plain to the eyes and boring in my dealings; people often "complain" that I am too focused on the task at hand. So why did Victor do that? I felt afraid and trapped... yet again. When his hands reached my breasts, I plunged into the sofa with Victor over me. I pushed back, and he fell to the floor with a moan and a dramatic frown on his face. I quickly used the opportunity to get up and wipe my mouth with the back of my hand. I explained I was sorry, that it was not my intention to provoke him or to push him to the floor… and I rectified "…I mean it was... but not to the floor…" I sounded like an idiot. I left his office, leaping to the door and dragging my heavy bag, muttering over and over again how sorry I was. And as I shut the door behind me, I was able to breathe… my heart still beating fast. My year as volunteer living in a RC's center in Barcelona, and my 17 years in RC had not prepared me to physically fight men.

Later that day, I presented my resignation.

I had thought Victor could be my mentor. I was desperate for one who would not want me for sex or cheap labor.

I found one shortly after that…

Chapter 3

ABSTINENCE

As I walked down Lexington Avenue, I tried to put my thoughts aside. I was almost at the pet store and somehow the "video clip" kept playing inside of my head like a movie trailer: *She was in the convent since she was 18. And, though while living the life of a 'nun' she did not lack opportunities...for several men had actually made passes at her, that day—at 37—Elena was practically a virgin.* The narrator's voice and the music ended as I entered the pet store.

"I'll take this one," I said to the clerk as I pointed at a small bed with my left hand, the same hand with which I was carrying my new puppy, covered with so much black fur that you could not even see his eyes. I visited that pet store often as I became reacquainted with what it was like to have a pet. The place was small and it smelled like dog, bird, and seaweed. In my right hand, I was carrying a Bloomingdales shopping bag with my latest acquisitions: a sleeping gown and jeans. I was proud of myself since I bought it all with over a 50 percent discount while the puppy slept peacefully inside of my purse. For the past 18 years I had worn long dresses or skirts, with slips and pantyhose underneath. Our bodies were always covered—even when we exercised or went to the beach, we wore shapeless, full-length skirts.

"That's a beautiful dog, a Shih tzu, right? Here... would you like to see a picture of the breed as adult?" the clerk asked as he opened a magazine on the counter.

"No!" I thought I probably sounded a bit irritated, so I felt the need to add with a soft tone and a smile, "No, thanks... it's not necessary." Expectations... a hindrance from the past—I carry some of my life's tendencies like a shackle tied to my ankle. "I don't want to condition the way I feel about the puppy to expectations," I continued. "I really don't care what the puppy will do, be, or look like when he grows..." That is what I wished those who had surrounded me in my life had said.

The clerk looked at me puzzled, and continued, "Alright... would you like anything else besides the bed?"

I gazed at the young clerk straight into the blue of his eyes... then my own eyes traveled through his face. *How old is he anyway, 20... maybe 30?* I couldn't even calculate. It shows what my approach towards the opposite sex was for years: Men without a wedding band were either young enough to be recruited for the Legion's seminary, or too old to join. The ones with a band were either rich enough to be benefactors, or too poor to contribute. Leaders enough to be invited to a retreat, or passive enough that attendance to a retreat wouldn't pay off. All other considerations were useless, or... inappropriate... potentially, a sin.

The voice of the young man became an echo in a back room inside my head. I could only see his blue eyes, his tanned skin, and a moving mouth. *A kiss...* how long had it been since I felt a kiss? It was better not to think about it—a strategy I learned while in RC, and surprisingly, it was still working. "The best way to avoid sin is to avoid the dialogue with the devil," my confessor reminded me once after I accused myself of longing for physical manifestations of affection. How I used to miss holding the hand of my childhood boyfriend... though that longing subsided with time. The feeling that never did was the longing for my father's strong hold... the way he would hug and squeeze me so tight that I used to have to raise my chin over his shoulder for air as I giggled, pleading to be released... And my mother's featherlike, sober, but constant kisses, and the ongoing teasing touch of my three brothers and three sisters—especially of my brothers, one older and two younger.

The young clerk stopped talking. His eyes were fixed on mine. Was he waiting for an answer? I could only remember he was asking if I needed something else besides the bed.

"Oh, yes! I will have food for the puppy, please."

"And what about the chewable treats and toys?" he asked.

"Oh, yes, please...Where do you have them?" I presumed that was what he was talking about while my mind wandered, thinking about my years of physical and affectionate abstinence... and his lips. Such a small puppy needed to keep his teeth busy on something other than my only decent shoes, a pair that I finally own. During 18 years, I wore *nunnish* black or brown shoes. They were dark, boring, and uncomfortable. For the first time in 18 years, I could wear delicate and colorful sandals–not as comfortable as I remembered them–but at least my toes were not compressed against a pointy, rubbery, imitation leather anymore... In RC, our budget rarely allowed for good quality shoes. And even when "directors" would give me a pair of shoes or anything else to wear, nothing was really mine. Things could disappear any day and be replaced by something else... if they were replaced at all.

I entered my modest studio apartment on 46th Street, a few blocks from the United Nations building, in Manhattan. The black ball squirmed around the floor, licking and sniffing everything he encountered. My therapist had suggested I should get a pet in order to open my heart to a less "conditioned" relationship where productivity was not a requirement. Productivity was the number one value for Father Maciel.

"What should I call you?" I asked the puppy. He stared back, tilting his head to one side and then the other, while I considered the pros and cons of several names. Then the tiny dog continued to lick and bite everything he found on his way through the apartment. I picked up an electricity bill that already had the canine's diminutive jaw printed all over it.

I called him Ricky, like Ricky Ricardo... I love Lucy had been one of my favorite shows growing up. I decided Ricky would remind me I was in the midst of a fun, fresh start. It was time to let go and move on, away from the Maciels and Victors of this world.

I placed Ricky's bed next to my air mattress as I explained to the pooch that the mattress was off limits, since I would end up on the floor or sleeping on his bed. All along I felt he could understand what I said... maybe due to the intensity of my need for company... or maybe because in some mysterious way, the cosmos feels pity on us humans who are lonely and gives us pets with special powers.

On one of the walls of the Manhattan studio, there was a very large window, the only window from which I could see the East River, and even Long Island. On the other side, there was a wall-to-wall mirror. I looked at myself often. Who would have thought it was so hard to put on weight? My appearance... I found it so hard to judge. My skin was still young; it was not white or dark. I suppose people could find it boring. I really truly wished I were attractive. *Does appearance help find friends? It cannot hurt...*When growing up, I never really tried to make friends. I was always surrounded by people: brothers, sisters, cousins, siblings' friends, cousins' friends, my friends, my nannies, other kids' nannies, chauffeurs, the nannies' and chauffers' kids, their kids' friends, cats, dogs, guinea pigs, horses, priests, and teachers. I often thought that I could do away with most people around me as long as I could keep my pets. Nevertheless, in RC, deprived of close friends for 18 years, I realized that to live without friends is one of the most painful things in life. We were taught that affective abstinence from everything and everyone "was the best way to keep one's heart available for God; Scripture says: 'we should love God with all our heart,' not with half the heart."

~ ~ ~ ~

Maciel looks at me from his throne. He is actually staring at me. He says, quoting Saint Augustine, "Elena, my dear, it is simple. God is Love. If you love, you can do as you like…"

"But you have always told us that the virgins of the Lamb will have a special place in heaven… for all eternity," I am desperate… he needs to understand why I hesitate. I am sitting at his feet and I look at him with surprised eyes. My gaze remains fixed on the man… the priest.

"Virginity is relative, Elena, it is a state of the soul, and it is for privileged souls like mine." His voice is solemn. He remains seated at the throne dressed in the traditional priestly outfit and wearing his artificially blond hair slicked back. He is now gazing at me with his kind and deep blue eyes as he strokes my hair. He then taps on his lap and nods. And when I stand, ready to act on his invitation and sit on him, I hear a moan, a cry.

I wake up and see black fur, a red tongue and two tiny paws on the edge of the bed. I cannot see the puppy's eyes, but from the sound of the cry he seems to say, "Pee... fast!" And, as I get up I pray like I do every morning:

God, I thank you for this day, I love you, and I need you!
If I have hurt someone, please forgive me.

Maciel never exactly seduced me… at least not in *that* way shown in my dream. During my last years in RC, rumors that Maciel had actually been a pedophile became common. For years, the Internet and the newspapers were censored in our centers. Everyone was "strongly advised" not to read or watch news that were not approved by superiors. And when I heard from a "stranger" outside of the community that there were new reports with new accusations regarding sex abuses, alleged drug addiction, and misuse of money, I at first discarded the thought. Nevertheless, at a later time I considered it. And when I shared my doubts with the directors, I was admonished—"Woman of little faith!" I left with my tail between my legs. Having been humiliated and embarrassed had not been unbearable. What burned, once again, like a hot iron on the chest, was feeling ashamed... not worthy... not enough. I betrayed them because I listened to my own judgment. I doubted a good man, a holy founder of the Church.

I stood for an instant in front of the wall-to-wall mirror. "I am OK," I told myself. I am hurting but alive, like the kitten.

When I heard a knock at the door I ran past the "living room" and "the foyer"—it was all the same room. And as I reached the apartment's door, a deathlike stench filled the air; it came from a box placed by my door. A neighbor was standing next to it, frowning with disgust. He informed me it had been there all night.

"Please, sweetie, can you get the package inside or get rid of it, or something? It smells all the way into our place," the man shrugged apologetically.

"I am sorry..." I said as I took it and I walked away from my apartment and into the fire stairs by the elevator. I didn't know what to expect but I could hardly stand the stink. I left it there and came back with a knife. I opened it. It was a bundle of brown paper, and inside was a dead black bird. I closed the box quickly, as if I could prevent the smell from slapping my face. I inhaled air and opened it again. I lifted the bird, careful to touch only the paper, and put it back; there was no note. I looked at the outside of the box... there was no name or address. I concluded it must have been a prank... *Of all people in the building, I got the dead blackbird... As if being deceived by Maciel had not been enough.*

The episode brought me back to another time in my life when I found a dead blackbird. It had been years ago. On that day, I spent the night in an abandoned Victorian-style house near Kankakee, Illinois. A family whose son was in the Legion, and whose daughter was considering joining RC, arranged for us to stay there. The house smelled like dust, sulfur, and dead meat. On that night in that house, with cracking floors and lockless knobs, I placed a mace spray on the table next to my bed. I was in one of the rooms on the second floor. I hardly slept. In the middle of the night I heard a cracking sound ascending the front wooden stairs. I took the mace and sat back on the bed. I prayed one of the most heartfelt prayers I have ever said in my life. I didn't scream so as not to expose my colleague who was sleeping in an adjacent room. The intruder retraced his steps and then I heard a door close. I had wanted to leave and spend the night driving but we couldn't; RC's rules indicated we could not be on the road past 9:00 p.m. In the morning, we found a dead blackbird outside my room.

Annoying coincidence.. but too many close calls! Two other times, I shared the house with homeless men without even knowing it. Both times, it had happened during the first days after we had purchased old abandoned homes to be used as new RC Centers or schools—one in Wakefield, Rhode Island, and the second one in Oxford, Michigan. Now, looking back, I know that had I been allowed to read the papers or hear the news with less "editing," I probably would have been more careful. Now and then, during "vocational recruitment" trips, I would hear people talk about terrible crimes committed against women who were in the wrong place at the wrong time... but since I was a *religious*, I felt impelled to foster trust in God, solace, and peace... so little thought was given to the unnecessary danger I exposed myself and my colleagues to during those years.

After securing the dead animal's stench inside of a couple of plastic bags, I deposited him in the garbage chute. I then ran to the computer. I had some research to do, and some people from "my past" that I needed to contact.

Chapter 4

SHAME

A dead blackbird could mean so many things: from a tribe's nickname to death. It all depended on the anonymous villain's background... *Great!* I remembered from my old-time travels across Oceania that there is a tribe in Queensland, Australia that is referred to as the Blackbird tribe. Native Aborigines even believe that birds carry stories. But then, I had also read that in the 19th century, blackbirding was the horrible practice of tricking, kidnapping, and trading slaves. And yet, in some early Christian writings, the blackbird is, like the snake, a symbol of evil. The devil had actually appeared to Saint Benedict in the form of a blackbird, tempter of the flesh.

It was probably all a coincidence. Nevertheless, I fathomed the possibility of being framed as either a dead tricked slave... or a trader of slaves. The latter turned my stomach inside out. While in the movement I had been tricked, as tricked as those who tricked me had been. Then, I learned to trick others without being aware that it was a trick. *Would my emails be enough to appease other victims?* No... but I still needed to write.

I thought of Rachelle...a woman who left our center to go back home during the summer candidacy program because she suffered a nervous breakdown. Had she forgiven me for sending her home? In hindsight, others would have been thankful. The day I put her on the plane, I received a call from the airline saying that she had "gotten off and got lost in Chicago," and did not catch the connecting flight to her hometown. She was found the next day. But then, Joe also came to mind: a young man who had been very upset because his girlfriend joined RC after one of my talks. And there was also a Canadian priest who would often stay at the same retreat house we did and had not taken my "preaching" nicely when I explained to him why he and I couldn't watch a movie together at his place. When I left RC, I received numerous notes where people expressed their affection and respect for me, and for my decision to leave; but then, there were some who resented me for trusting in Maciel blindly and introducing them to RC. Could they have sent me the dead blackbird? How would they know where I lived?

After spending some time at the computer replying to kind notes of support and reaching out to others who had left, I turned my attention to Ricky—when you don't have a backyard, it feels like dogs need to pee all the time. After walking him, I left him in the apartment, and I also left the ghost of the bird's stench walking the hallways of the building. I headed towards the gym.

I needed to recover my physical and mental health. The demands of my life in RC and the conflicts my conscience constantly endured left me thin as a rag and tired—physically and emotionally exhausted. During my last months in the movement, I had begun to suffer temporary episodes where I would lose my memory. "Amnesia at 35 is not normal," I told my director once, asking yet again if I could see a doctor. But doctors would always repeat the same thing: "You are just tired."

Once at an airport, somewhere in New Zealand, I felt so sick that I sat in the terminal's corner and wept, and slept. Many people approached me that day, asking if I needed help. I stayed there for hours throughout the night. Then, instead of catching my 13-hour plane somewhere, I took public transportation to the nearest beach, small bag in hand. I was there all day eating from a peanut butter jar. Thank God I had asked the nuns at the last convent where I stayed if I could keep the jar. It was the end of a long trip and I had been left with some dollars but used it for the bus. I scooped the peanut butter out with my index finger, against RC's strict etiquette rules. *Why did it feel so good to defy a simple rule? Why were there so many rules in RC, anyhow?* And sitting on a rock with my long skirt rubbing against the sand, I never got tired of observing the surfers. I decided I would just be a surfboard and enjoy floating—not swimming—and the rhythm of the waves. At the end of that day, I went back to the airport to beg the airline agent to put me on the next flight to Los Angeles; I was stationed in Pasadena. With no money, no credit cards, and a USA Religious Visa, plus no permit to reside in New Zealand, it had been easy to have my wishes granted.

I entered the Equinox Gym at Grand Central Terminal and signed up. "I can deprive myself of other things, but I can't afford to skip food, sleep, and exercise," I whispered to myself as I signed the contract and squinted my eyes with determination. I was now left with no "extra" money. "You don't have a budget to get sick or to heal a toothache," I whispered again to myself. Needless to say, I did not have health insurance at that point. I knew my father would give me more money if I really needed it, but I did not want to have to ask.

I went into a Zumba class and surrendered completely to the task of getting my muscles back and, why not, my figure and my happiness.

My long T-shirt and baggy pants contrasted with the spandex and tight outfits everyone else— mostly women—wore. I took note to purchase some gym outfits at St. Jeanne's Thrift store at the corner of 77th and Lexington. Somehow, residents from the Upper East Side in Manhattan donated new and beautiful clothes to St. Jeanne's Church. When I was young, I would purchase my clothes in Houston, in expensive stores at the Galleria; now I was getting clothing for a couple of dollars at a thrift store, and furniture at Goodwill—a financially healthy habit I have not lost 15 years later, even with a steady and well-paid job.

After the class, in the dressing rooms, women of all ages undressed by their lockers with no shame. They threw the towel over their shoulders and walked to the showers or sauna, topless or everything-less. They spoke about their trips, their newest acquisitions, or gossiped about men at work. They even compared notes or asked about different birth control methods, without a worry about who was listening. *There are no spies in their world, no team balances, and no superiors who would give penances or punishments for having offended God.* One of the most shameful and poisonous of all activities in RC was the "team-balance." We had it every other week. It was an opportunity to exercise "fraternal correction." "Tell your sisters, in Christian charity, what they have done wrong. When you do it, explain why it is wrong using what is written in our 'statutes' and code of conduct." I heard all sorts of "justified" criticisms and judgments on my colleague's actions and my own actions during that biweekly hour. Everyone in the community had to participate, except for superiors or "directors" of the center, and Maciel. In RC, criticizing a superior constituted a grave fault. At the gym, I could see and hear and not have to tell tales on anyone. Actually, while in the movement I had exercised "fraternal correction" during team balance a few times and had felt so bad that I never did it again. Of course, my decision to not participate during team balance had not gone unnoticed. Someone had then corrected me: "Elena, you don't say anything regarding anyone during team balance and it shows you don't care about your sisters' improvement and perfection."

I walked into the sauna with a towel around my body. The heat enveloped me completely. It felt like an embrace. I took a seat on one of the benches in the back. The mist made it hard to see but I sensed the presence of one, maybe two women on the opposite side… naked. One was lying down with her stomach on the bench; the other was sitting next to her and leaning back against one of the sidewalls with her legs bended over the bench. I made a point to keep my eyes closed until I heard a moan. I opened my eyes and realized the women were… touching. More than touching. I quickly closed my eyes again. Guilt hit… a familiar feeling. I tried hard to remove the image of what I had just seen from my mind… then I heard a young but low voice say from the sauna door, "Give me a break! Get a room!" When I opened my eyes again I saw the women who had been on the bench leaving the sauna, dragging their towels behind them, and as they passed through the door where the outspoken young woman stood, they gave her a piercing look.

I was unable to close my eyes again. Every time I did, the scene of the women with the face of one on the other's crotch played like a video clip projected in the interior of my eyelids… and something behind my bellybutton would stir. I had not been touched even in a chaste way in 18 years. I had not even touched myself. I studied about chastity in my classes when I was in RC. I also meditated on the virtue using Father Maciel's epistles. In the movement, we had to meditate on the founder's letters during 30 minutes every day. In his letters, Maciel spoke extensively about chastity. He would explain it as abstinence from all physical and emotional intimacy with everything other than God himself. It was, therefore, a superior virtue, superior to human love. "Abstinence and sexual control will free you in order to love more, love better with the spirit," Maciel wrote in one of the letters he sent me. I repeated it every time the "feeling" of longing inside of me would emerge. I was not sure where the physical sensation resided—I did not want to explore or even think about it. I repeated Maciel's words constantly as if they had the power to become true.

Once, overcoming a horrible sense of shame, I summoned up the courage to confess to Maciel the difficulties I was having in "that" area… meaning "chastity." I explained I would wake up aroused in the mornings and was insolent enough to think for an instant that I could make a spouse very happy—of course, that is, if I were to leave the movement, which I considered constantly. "You are… your interior is like a balloon…" Maciel started to say, apparently red with anger and lacking the words. And finally, releasing his breath at once, he exclaimed with a soft and tender voice, "You are like a balloon inflated with selfishness. God never asks for something unless he gives you the strength needed to correspond to his request!" I nodded and kept quiet. I understood and believed in what Maciel said. I did not question God's coherence. My silenced question was: How could Maciel be certain of what God wanted from me? Was it God, or was Maciel imposing his will and judgment on me? In RC, the superiors represented God's will, and this fusion of God and man hindered our ability to listen to the voice of our own conscience.

There was another time when I talked to Maciel about a similar difficulty, though this one had to do with "friendships and affections"— nothing physical. Maciel's line of questioning surprised me. "What do you mean? But... what do you exactly feel?" Maciel asked as if he had been delving in the descriptions and expected a greater and more detailed explanation. "And... are you working on a regular basis with this...'person'?" I was confessing the fact that I liked being with a male coworker, and I thought we should be allowed to be friends. But Maciel spent too much time talking and asking about our physical contact. He told me I needed to be vigilant and keep the flesh punished and under control. "Do you like him?" *"Yes, I like him."* "Are you left alone with him sometimes?" *"No."* "And what would you do if you were alone?" *"Nothing."* "Does he like you too? *No... I mean, yes... normal. Maybe he likes me as well, but not like that."* "Like what?" *"Like a boyfriend... we're just friends.... I know it is wrong to be friends... No, I don't think of him naked... No... He is just a friend...I mean, I like him as a friend!"* My cry was silent. I couldn't show my tears. They would be misinterpreted.

In RC, consecrated women could never meet a man alone or travel by themselves. The rule indicated we had to be accompanied by a "woman colleague" at all times, and this person would be chosen and assigned by the director of the community. In general, I followed that rule to the letter... so definitively there was not much to tell Maciel. I concluded that maybe he was asking because he could see something I couldn't. He was "a saint" after all. Maciel thought that my feelings of arousal in the mornings were related to my closeness to this coworker.

Looking back, it is not surprising. What else can be expected from a serial rapist? I was sure it would mean the end of my work relationship with this person. Most likely Maciel would transfer me or remove me from my assignment... or would remove him. It was too late; I had opened up. I tried to be faithful by being honest, but Maciel's opinion of me would plunge. That was the price I had to pay for showing my fragility. I was contaminated. A very familiar sadness took over my heart once again, squeezing my breath out.

On that occasion, Maciel did not transfer me to a different city. He had not even given orders to change my duties; instead, that afternoon my confessor handed me a little black cloth bag. Inside there was a belt made out of wires and sharp nail-like spikes with a leather cord at both ends. "It is called a cilice," he explained, and told me to wear it every day for several months. "Place it like a belt under your skirt, around one of your thighs. You can also place it on your waist, but it might be more practical to wear it on the thigh since you will make it tighter when you see... *him*."

Next time my coworker and I met to work, things had not been the same. I could hardly concentrate that afternoon. The sting I felt on the thigh was constant and penetrating. I was afraid to move, to stand, to sit. I was wearing nylons. The women in RC were required to wear nylons to cover our legs... always... every day, all day.

I wore the cilice on the left thigh, under the nylons, for two years. I also wore a long slip and the blood of the wound from the metal spikes would not show on the skirt. It wouldn't drip either since it coagulated on the nylon. The burning sensation worsened in the heat when the salty sweat would penetrate the wound. Removing the slip and nylons would rip the scar open over and over again. "Abstinence of all expressions of physical love is a superior form of love," I would remember Maciel's words and whisper them as if I was apologizing to my body for punishing it with pain and bleeding. "Had you joined RC younger, you wouldn't be tormented by temptations in this way," Maciel had also said that day. According to him, the younger one joined, the better—less of a chance for contamination. It was, therefore, a common practice in RC to recruit boys who were as young as 11 and girls at 14. For me, it had been almost 19.

I was exhausted from the heat of the sauna and the memories. Looking down at my legs, I could see the scars left by the cilice right below the towel. I stood, secured my towel around my body, and left.

When I returned home, Ricky welcomed me. He was truly a happy puppy and I felt jealous. I wanted to be cared for and not used. But, would I know how to live like that? Could I experience happiness simply because I "was," with no added-on expectations?

I needed to get a job that would pay my single-life bills. I thought about many of my friends, married to wealthy men, and I felt scared. I did not want to "belong" to someone anymore. I thought of my parents' love for each other, and the way they belonged to themselves in most ways… I knew I should have gone back home to re-learn from them how to make relationships work, but the fear of not meeting everyone's expectations won, and I stayed far away… It was a grave mistake that—as I later learned—had grave consequences.

Chapter 5

Team Balance

After uploading my resume on several job-search engines on the Internet, I got up and stretched, raising my arms and arching my back. I had not been allowed to do that in RC. Once I stretched in my bedroom. It had been a room shared by two other consecrated women. Members would need to share bedrooms in most centers due to shortage of space—and it was all right to do so, as long as there were three or more in the same room, never two since it was conducive to confidences and could be a source of temptation. Typically, two bunk beds plus one bed would do it. The center's director would assign shower turns; two would shower in the morning—in different turns of course—and two or three at night. We were still expected to be ready in less than half an hour… No doubt a man—Maciel –and not us, had set that rule. No one was allowed to speak in the bedrooms. All speaking among members had to be done in common areas. That week, during team-balance, I was accused of lacking temperance and fostering lust in the act of stretching my body in the bedroom. My shock had not gone unnoticed. I tried to smile, but inside, the emotional distance and distrust between my roommate and me grew. Had the "team balance" been a strategic move on Maciel's part to foster distrust among us? After all, it was natural to avoid confidentiality and intimacy when everyone around you was motivated to judge your actions and announced them publicly. Team balance accomplished two goals important to Maciel: tattletaling, which facilitates control; and emotional distance, which avoids confidences. Avoiding confidentiality is crucial in preventing upheaval and revolt.

~ ~ ~ ~

I see myself in the Legion's Seminary for priests in Thornwood, outside of Manhattan. I recognize the conference room. I met there with Maciel on numerous occasions, especially when he wanted to analyze how rapidly RC was growing. He attended those meetings with the bimonthly reports that everyone had to turn in indicating what we were doing to make RC bigger and more successful every day; that is, what we did "to give God glory." I hear Maciel's voice: "He or she who does not give life, kills. He who does not make RC grow, is a parasite. He who is not with me is against me." Out of the corner of my eye, I see him walking into the room. Everyone stands; the judge has entered the courtroom. He carries in his hand not the reports, but a bunch of cilices as if they were a bouquet of flowers. He wears a black double-breasted suit, as he and all priests in the Legion do. His hair is fake blond and is combed in its usual slicked-back manner. His blue eyes sweep the room. My eyes do the same. I recognize some people. They are colleagues from RC.

"Alright," Maciel says as he paces in the front of the room, and in between the rows of desks that the participants occupy like school kids. "Rosa," he says addressing one of the women, "since you have only gotten five new inductees this year, I will give you one of these to wear. No doubt your lack of apostolic results, of recruits, is due to your laziness and your distractions. This will help you keep your soul and mind vigilant." Rosa takes the cilice with a bright smile as he hands it to her. She smells it as if were an actual flower. Maciel continues to scrutinize the room as he walks towards me. "Like father, like daughter," he says standing right in front of my face. "That is why you are successful, Elena. But your vanity destroys your purity, so lift your skirt and lower your nylons." At what looks like center stage, I do as he orders. I quickly let go of my skirt—I do not want to show my horrendous white cotton underwear. Maciel hands me the entire bouquet of cilices, keeping one in his hand. He takes it and wraps it around my left thigh. My nylons are scrunched on my knees. Maciel

pulls the cilice's strings to make the spiky belt even tighter around my leg. The flesh breaks-open and starts to bleed. My hand instinctually tightens the grip and now I start to feel those spikes cutting through my fingers as well. My breath accelerates.

I woke up.

I was sweating—my fingers were in Ricky's playful jaw.

When, in real life, I had those meetings—in that same room—in order to "measure the authenticity of my love for God" with the number of recruits, I felt ashamed. And the shame I felt in the dream, when I raised my skirt for Maciel to place a cilice on my bare leg, now I knew, was not any worse.

The fact that I have a strong character is probably attributed to my genetics... "Like father, like daughter." But why only celebrate its advantages and not its challenges? I got a lot of heat from Maciel at times because I spoke my mind. One day, for example, he cancelled his trip for a meeting I organized in Rhode Island with a few hundred people. I got upset. Who could understand that the trip from Mexico City to Rhode Island, on a private plane I managed to get for him, was cancelled because he was expected to fly with other passengers? His secretary informed me that *Nuestro Padre,* as many in the Church call founders, flies accompanied by his secretary and no one else.

"Are you telling me that you don't want him to share the private jet with its owners?" I had shouted on the phone.

"That's right," the secretary said. "And you better go to confession for the way you are speaking to me."

"It's not worse than how you speak to me, Father," I had screamed back before hanging up the phone.

Beggars can't be choosers. I contrasted what I heard on the phone with Mother Teresa of Calcutta's life. The tiny wrinkled nun and I had met once on a public bus in Rome. She was holding tight to a pole, sustaining a smile as the crowded bus swung her around, bouncing back and forth in the midst of passengers. The toughest part was that I could not speak about it. But since I needed an explanation badly—something that would show me how such apparent arrogance and holiness could coexist—I opened up and expressed my frustration to my director, breaking the rule of silence to never criticize a superior or their decisions. "It is a matter of charism," the director said. "We have a different calling. We are called to be efficient in our work and the secretary is probably considering that *Nuestro Padre* needs to rest or work during the trip. Time is Christ's Kingdom."

> I jumped out of bed and started the day with my usual prayer:
> *God, I thank you for this day, I love you, and I need you!*
> *If I have hurt someone, please forgive me.*

I had received two email messages in response to one of my Internet posts. In my brief note, I had written I was looking for answers and for forgiveness from those I introduced to RC. One of them read:

Hello, Elena—I am the granddaughter of someone who knew Marcial Maciel ("Marcialito") well, as a child. My grandfather worked on Maciel's ranch. Now that he is very old, he spends many hours in bed telling me stories. Many of them, I believed to be fiction... But as Maciel's alleged abuses became public I began to wonder.

My grandfather tells the story of how Maciel was 10 when one of his father's young workers started to "play" sex with him. Papa sheds tears every time he tells me the story. He says that Marcialito did not have a chance... that he was abused by some of the older workers when they realized the boys' game.

According to my grandfather, Maciel endured the abuses for two or three years... until one day... when something inside him changed. It was as if the boy built a shield around his soul. "The boy was darn smart," my grandfather says... "And he learned to play by his own rules."

There you have it. I guess one can say Maciel learned to take control of the pain... before the pain controlled him. Good luck in your quest for forgiveness, healing, and peace.

The second one was from a woman I will call Becca, who was 106 at the time. Her niece was writing for her. She explained in detail how Maciel would visit her town in 1954, driving his uncle's 1950s Ford. His uncle was a bishop and allegedly, Maciel was helping him find vocations to the priesthood. She then explained in detail how their town was special since, during the Cristero War, the religious persecution that Mexico endured in the 1920s and 1930s, it produced holy men and women who defended their right to profess their faith.

Becca's nephew had joined RC at 11, and soon after that, Maciel abused him sexually for three months. It hadn't been as simple as it sounds... Joachim, Becca's nephew, had not told anyone, it was Becca who experienced a strong intuition and got him out of the minor seminary right away.

She explained that her intuition could be attributed to her Mayan and Gaelic ancestors. She was the descendant of an Irish prisoner among the many who nationalized as Mexicans when they deserted the USA and the British Army during the war against their fellow Catholic Mexicans... he was one of the only lucky ones who survived the war. According to her, she knew her intuition was factual the minute she visited Joachim, and so... she did not allow him to stay at the seminary. After she got some of the facts from Joachim, she wrote to the local Catholic bishop, since Joachim was too embarrassed to go to the police. The bishop replied saying that it was the word of the priest against the word of the boy.

> "Year after year, I saw families escorting their children to Maciel's car and giving them their parental blessing. I knew some of them, I knew those parents would give their lives for their young boys, and yet, they were sending them

to a living hell. Year after year, I warned them but yet again… it was my word against that of the priest. Maciel, by the way, managed to make up stories against Joachim and me, and people believed him… he was quite a charismatic man, that evil man. As time passed and the order grew, the deafness of those warned grew as well. And very soon, with so much power, there was little anyone could do.

So if someone needs to apologize, sweet child, it is not you but I… for not running to warn your parents—and all parents—the day you left to join Maciel and his order. But then… would they have listened?"

After that, I could not read any more. Instead, I prepared for a meeting with a man someone had suggested was willing to be my mentor.

Chapter 6

DESTINY

I see destiny as the fusion of my heart's desires and heaven's gifts. To reach this belief, my soul had to go through regeneration. I had to do away with the black-and-white concept of: "God's will is the director's will"… or "If you do not do God's will, you will not be happy." I began by praying about God's essence, trying to understand God's nature as much as I could and concluding that our heart's deep desires are in essence good, and that his gifts will always surround us… they are not conditioned to our limited vision constrained by time and personality. Therefore, destiny is the fusion of our heart's desires and heaven's gifts. When we open a door in our life—out of free will—as long as it is not a crime… it is never a "good" or a "bad" door… it is just a door, and behind every door, there is a gift waiting. That lesson is one I learned not during those years, but looking back after almost two decades of healing.

Destiny brought me to live in Manhattan. I believe I stayed in the USA because I desired to have a family and a career, and I thought that if I went back to Monterrey, my possibilities of finding someone to marry that—at the same time—would "set me free," were scarce. This is a topic I will expand on later.

Around the time I settled in New York City, in January of 2002, even though I had not gone to school yet for my doctoral degree, I started to watch TV shows with a researcher's attitude—something I still do. I had missed almost two decades of pop culture and it was affecting my socialization. I didn't know what *Seinfeld*, *Friends*, *Pee-Wee*, Super Mario, or *Cheers* were. I had not seen *Back to the Future*, *Terminator*… not even *The Princess Bride*—my favorite movie of all time. I had no idea who Tom Cruise or Brat Pitt were; and I still don't know most of the actors' and actresses' names from the 1980s and 1990s.

At the beginning, when I started going out with acquaintances—neighbors or other dog-owners—I couldn't follow some conversations. Between the double-meaning jokes, the references to pop culture, and certain idiomatic expressions, I was constantly guessing and asking for clarification. Later, I would constantly make embarrassing mistakes such as saying "I will bend over for you" (instead of "I will bend over backwards"), or "cut the cheese" (instead of "cut to the chase"). Unless the theme was related to education, geography, history, philosophy, or theology, I had a hard time following the conversation. My acquaintances were good people who used young adult vocabulary... and though in RC I had matured professionally and intellectually, in every other way, I was still 18.

In one of my TV pop culture research sessions I saw, for the first time, an ad from the Humane Society asking for donations to help abused pets. The screen showed a dog in a cage withdrawing into a corner as HS staff reached out to him. It was obvious that the dog distrusted and that experience was telling him it was better to withdraw. At the same time, if the dog could speak, he would probably cry: "What I desire the most is what I craved for so long until I got used to being deprived... until it hurt so much to desire, so I don't desire any longer." It reflected my own sentiments. In my case, I knew I could learn to trust again because by nature I am an idealist—in my world, the sky is the limit, and I always give people the benefit of the doubt—an attribute which currently makes me good at my job as teacher-preparation faculty. But when it came to matters of the heart... of *my* heart, Maciel's statement would haunt me: "No human love will satisfy you." I had learned not to expect intimacy and to be afraid of that expectation. That scar later led me to choices that produced a great deal of sorrow.

One of them was choosing to remain in the USA, away from Monterrey and my family.

Since... still... destiny is the fusion of my choices and gifts from heaven, after choosing to stay in New York, heaven sent me one of the greatest gifts I have received in my life: Cole. Cole had a successful career as a schoolteacher and district administrator, before putting everything on the line to fight corruption in schools. When he retired, he co-founded Educational Innovation-Public Education Association, a nonprofit that supports public education in New York City. He spent his life seeing the potential in his students and everyone around him, and acting upon it so they could see their bright future for themselves. When I met him, he spent 45 minutes with me outside of a New York public school in Harlem. Not once did he look at his watch. Not once did he ask me to do something for him. He listened and responded to my intense questions with lightness of heart. The advice he gave me that day was—not only right, as I later discovered—but "free of charge." He didn't want money or work in return... very different from what I had experienced in RC.

Some days later, Cole and I were sitting at a large round table, side-by-side. The occasion was a fundraising event organized by his nonprofit organization. The rest of the guests were dancing to some jazzy live music.
"I wish you could see your potential. If you don't believe in yourself, no one will, Elena."
I took another sip of red wine and leaned back in the chair. I remember feeling pretty that night. I had started to put makeup on for the first time in almost two decades. Cole looked at me incredulously. "OK, I'm not convincing you, am I?" I didn't have the opportunity to reply since, as I thought about my answer, I got distracted with a

request from a waiter, while a beautiful petite woman asked Cole to dance.

I spent the rest of the night conversing with other guests and dancing. After the band announced they would play the last melody, I got my coat and headed towards the door. Cole joined me.

"Come with me tomorrow," he said as he held the taxi door open. "Actually, it's not a question. I need you to come with me tomorrow. Tomorrow at 9 a.m., at the corner of 116th and Lexington."

"Alright," I said as I got in a taxi.

Chapter 7

AN ANGEL

At 116th Street and Lexington... that meant I needed to take subway number 6 (the Lexington Avenue line), going uptown in Manhattan from 42nd Street (Grand Central) to 116th Street on the local train—give or take a 10-minute ride. I love that about Manhattan. It is practically impossible to get lost—helpful for someone like me with absolutely no sense of direction but a good memory for maps. Numbered streets are horizontal strips, and the vertical line that divides them into east and west is 5th Avenue which, like the rest of the roads going south to north and vice versa, are avenues.

One of my most well-known spiritual attributes—partly from life experiences—is my connection to the dead, or my faith in the "communion of the saints." After so many years on the road, traveling for RC, I got used to memorizing maps. So every time, I closed my eyes to see the map of Manhattan in my head, I thanked the deceased engineers who designed the city. Eventually, that led me to research. The designers were not the Dutch who arrived in the 16th century and bought the land from the natives for nothing, nor the English who attempted to take it over in the 18th century. After the War of Independence, Manhattan residents, skilled inhabitants who were carefully selected and financially and morally motivated to do the best job they could were commissioned to plan it. And that definitively explains why they did such a good job.

Another thing I loved about living in Manhattan was that I did not need a car. After my endless road and plane trips in RC, I disliked most wheel-supported vehicles, leaving room for snowmobiles, hot air balloons, and some trains... plus horses, for that matter.

There was a mixed crowd at the busy 116th intersection in East Harlem. It was Monday morning and most people were heading to work, but some lingered on the corners, waiting for a business transaction—marijuana or heroin, most likely. There were a few public high schools nearby which sadly turned the neighborhood into a drug negotiation arena.

"Hello, beaueau-t-t-tiful teach-cher." The words sputtered out of a man's mouth, inches from my face. His vodka breath felt hot on my cheek.

I probably did look like a teacher with my navy blue pencil skirt, three-button jacket, flats and a red tank top underneath the suit as a funky factor to avoid feeling nunnish. I offered a shy smile, holding the expensive—once-upon-a-time my mother's—leather handbag close to my chest. To be drunk in the morning was not unusual among the homeless men and women in Manhattan, for whom regular day-to-day life was a teacup ride they had chosen not to get on. Some, when sober or alert, would jump in for a while but then, when the dizziness from the spinning of daily commitments became unbearable, they would jump right out again. While out of the game, the day-to-night cycle would turn into something they could simply contemplate, instead of partake in. This drunken man had definitively been exempt from the teacup ride all night and all morning so far. I knew I had nothing to worry about as long as I held tight to my purse. If something serious were to happen, at least dozen individuals—commuting to work—would come to my rescue... 9/11 had made New Yorkers more caring. Besides, with my dark brown hair pulled back in a loose ponytail and my tan skin, I fit in.

"Maybe we should walk this gentleman to the soup kitchen on Third Avenue. He can use a dark coffee and a sturdy breakfast." Cole appeared looking freshly shaved and smelling good. He tried holding the man by the arm.

"My sweet gen-tle-man. I do not need drrrr-ak coffee. I just need money." The man displayed a line of yellow teeth framed by a fake smile, and weakly jerked his arm away from Cole.

"Alright." Cole let go of the man and addressed his full attention to me. "You look nice, professional," he added checking my outfit briefly.

Though I preferred other clothes—as different from the clothes I had worn in RC as possible—I accepted that I would have to wear professional clothes once in a while.

"Hi to you too," I said, and he smiled.

We walked east on 116th Street. "Today, we will see a dear friend, a former colleague, who really wants to meet you."

"Her name is Evelyn Castro," he continued nonchalantly. He was definitively comfortable in his own skin. "Just be yourself. She might ask you some questions... Okay, let's say that she might want to hire you." Cole sighed, and stopped to look at me intently. "Elena, actually, this is a job interview. I hope you don't mind."

Mind? I was ecstatic, but nervous. I still found it strange that someone would do such a kind act without any institutional or personal benefit.

"Let's see how it goes. Keep an open mind, alright?" he said.

"You are incredible! You do this out of the goodness of your heart!" I believe I was trying to provoke an answer.

"I'm not sure what that means, but here in 'the world,'" quotation marks gestured, "everything people do is preceded by a motivation." And then, he added matter-of-factly, "There is both an institutional and personal benefit." No, Cole was not reading my mind; he was referring to a conversation we had some days back, where I had questioned the legitimacy of utilitarianism. He continued: "If you are hired by Evelyn, it is only because she needs you and you are the best candidate for the opening; if that happens, the East Harlem School District benefits... that is the institutional benefit. And many people benefit, especially you... that is the personal benefit. I benefited years back when someone put a good teacher on my path. It's my turn to pay it forward. So remember that there is always a motivation—it's part of being human… and there's nothing wrong with that. The key is: there has to be an understanding between adults; the motivation is overtly known by both parties, and it's something both seek, want, and accept."

Life later taught me, through Peter Senge, an inspired expert on Systems Thinking, that a worthwhile personal vision and mission is always something that you seek for its own sake, because of its own worth. The clearest example of this is parents' dedication to their child, or artists' creation of art. So the world does work based on certain pragmatic principles after all: pragmatism in relation to values. A value that is overt and agreed upon. But even then, though fair and legal, it is not always moral. An old lady could give everything—donate her entire estate to RC—to the point of depriving herself of essentials. Her motivation and value were overt and agreed upon: "I want to give all my money to you… you want to receive all of it." It might be legal and fair, but it is not moral for the person receiving the gift to receive it all if the old lady might need it for her survival. I knew of at least one woman in that situation, in my hometown of Monterrey. She gave more than what she could afford, and RC accepted it. I had also freely surrendered my will and judgment to Maciel, and it had been immoral for him to accept my blind obedience. It was immoral for me to renounce to my judgment—something so vital for a human to survive as a human and not as a slave.

"I've been looking for someone like you. As you probably know, there is a very large population of immigrants in this area; they speak mostly Spanish and some of them speak French. It's been hard to find someone who can speak both and who will understand their situation. Students are required to learn English, but it's not always possible for the parents to learn it." Evelyn was a middle-aged, bright woman from Puerto Rico. Cole and Evelyn's friendship was almost as old as their careers. Her office was a rectangle with an equally rectangular window overseeing a rectangular... cement area. "Besides, you seem to have the necessary background to acquire a New York State teaching certification," Evelyn added, scanning my postgraduate credits. "And if you have credits pending, there are amazing universities around where you can get them. Of course, if you are interested."

I hesitated. Teaching was at the top of my career options but I was not exactly an immigrant—was I? I had been raised in a well-to-do family, and though I was fluent in English and Spanish, I had learned academic French while attending an all-girls boarding school in California... not exactly the French I would hear in the streets of Harlem.

By the end of the visit, I had accepted the job. Before that interview, I had not spent enough time thinking about my identity, a topic that surrounds me now, as I do my doctoral dissertation. Identity is ever changing and thus, I realized I had become a Mexican-American immigrant in the US. In addition, though I mostly held administrative jobs in RC, I simultaneously and mainly was always a teacher and a professor. My happiest moments had involved teaching, innovating solutions, researching, and organizing information—all transferable skills that I have maximized in my life and that definitively mark out my identity as a professor. Accepting a New York City teaching job was the perfect gift that would pave the path towards many other gifts as an educator. Very soon after that, and after taking a few courses at Fordham and Hunter College, New York State validated my degree in education, many of my credits in languages, and granted me certificates as an ESL (English as a Second Language), Spanish, and bilingual teacher.

Everything in my life began to take shape. Coleman continued to guide me in my professional life, especially when it came to navigating politics and the bureaucratic system. I also had the opportunity to meet his wife and I realized it had been the beautiful petite woman who had asked him to dance during his nonprofit event. She was as smart and as caring as Cole.

By the fall of 2002, I was happily teaching ESL and assisting the district's Bilingual Education Director in numerous tasks. Not only was my job perfect, but my commute to work was, too. In Manhattan it takes an average walker one minute to walk one block—north or south. The formula does not apply when you walk east to west, or vice versa. Distance between avenues is not as predictable… but it averages two minutes per avenue: delightful information for a geek like me. So invariably, it would take me an hour to walk to work, or about a 20-minute subway ride.

There was only one aspect of my life where I still felt lost: I did not know how to incorporate my past as "a nun" within my present professional and social life. At the beginning, I would speak about it until I realized it created awkward moments and prejudices. When I went out with a new friend, there was a "Hi, I made a reservation…at x place for dinner," followed by a walk or a cab ride with small talk. And then, the inevitable question: "Tell me about yourself. " The minute I mentioned I had been in "a movement"… almost a cult, the conversation would zoom in and the interrogation would start. People tend to think that you are not as smart if you ended up fooled by Maciel, or that maybe you have terrible emotional needs since people who go into cults are desperate for a community. As a RC victim, you have been trained to put the blame on yourself, so interactions with people who inevitably judge you are incredibly hurtful, not to mention harmful.

Another challenge was indecisiveness. Like most young adults, you are anxious to give love a chance, and you know you should not ignore the longing to love. However, the habit of relying on others as the ultimate decision makers leads you to freeze up and be indecisive. My heart was not showing what direction to go in, and I did not have a superior who could tell me what to do. My friend Cole was not very helpful either. The thought of making a mistake terrified me. Once married, there would be no second chances... or would there be?

One day, I finally got a straight answer from Cole, a friendly word of advice regarding life-partner choice. He looked pale and had lost weight. "A bad cold," he explained. "So while I was sick and in bed, I had time to think about your question and this is what I would say: Be patient and don't rush. You will go through several adjustments and phases and you will develop reference points. Most likely, if you rush and decide in haste, you will make a mistake."

Only one year after that conversation, the day Cole was buried, I remembered it with deep pain and love. Respiratory complications and chemo, not a cold, drained Cole's life. Illness had taken him away... too soon. As I watched the coffin descend into the ground's mouth, I reflected on how his life had been suddenly transferred to a different world, and how much I detested separation. "Bye... and thanks," I whispered to his soul as the sun went down that afternoon. He had become more than my mentor; he was my angel. The temptation to complain to God was washed away when I realized I had at least enjoyed him and loved him during one year. Had his illness taken him a year earlier, Cole's life and mine would not have crossed. My gift was to have met him. It was up to me now to live what I learned from my one-year angel.

Chapter 8

TRAPPED

I woke up before sunrise, wet in my own sweat. I was in Palm Beach, Florida, in a somehow, somewhat familiar room. At least, that is where I had been in my dream. It was the same place where I "rested" for a week under my superiors' orders a couple of years before I left RC.

Palm Beach had not been an inconvenience. I actually loved the beach. What bothered me was the assumption that simple rest could stop the deterioration of my health. I was trying to eat and take care of myself but my body was starting to shut down.

Often, when one of us had signs of extreme stress, superiors in the Legion would send us to rest for a few days or weeks, in a "happy place." Palm Beach definitely qualified, but at the same time, it reminded me of some of the aspects that I could not accept about RC. For example, while the priests could wear their bathing suit on the beach, we had to wear our clothes over it, and take them off only while swimming. I cannot remember what exactly triggered my temporary exile to Palm Beach but it had been spur of the moment. I arrived to the center in Greenville, RI after a long road trip, and I was called to the director's office.

"You are leaving tomorrow for Palm Beach to rest and you are going with Claudia. We already have the tickets and you will need to find a hotel or motel room to stay in when you get there. Ask the taxi driver; they always know where to go if you give them a price range."

"And what is my price range?"

"Claudia knows."

As always, I thanked her and left her office. I went straight to my room to unpack but then realized there was no need since I was leaving again the following day. I just opened the luggage and put in the one-piece bathing suit.

Something similar happened to one of my coworkers. She had been sent to rest because, according to superiors, she was too tired and her mind was playing tricks on her. She had confided to her director that she saw Father Maciel outside of Boston's airport getting into a luxurious car, driven by a chauffeur in uniform. Maciel was accompanied by two young women... one very young. She explained that Maciel had placed his hand on the buttocks of one of the women, giving her a gentle spank... something you don't do to the wife of a benefactor. It was a woman Maciel had introduced in Mexico to a group of us as a benefactor's wife, together with her daughter. My coworker was scolded for allowing those thoughts and was told that it was her imagination before she was sent away to "rest." As it turns out, it had been in fact Maciel, and the women traveling with him were his hidden mistress and their 20-year-old daughter. I learned about this incident once both my coworker and I had left RC. While in the movement, we couldn't share our suspicions with each another.

I think we all came to question the promise to never criticize superiors. For me it was 1997, when my father had a stroke that almost took his life and my superiors did not tell me until days later because they needed me to continue with my plans to take a group of students to Rome for a RC celebration. I began to distance myself emotionally from RC after that. That healthy "distance," in addition to rest and maturity—I was 33 years old at the time—led me to begin to reverse the brainwashing that had started when I was a teen.

Despite the fact that I was stubborn and rebellious in many ways, the superiors always tried to convince me to stay and not abandon the movement. They said it was God's will for me to stay, that I had a vocation to consecrated life "greater than a cathedral." They would tell me I was "gifted." Literally, they would use the word *valiosa*, or "of value." I presume that the fact that my father was a benefactor was also a motivation. Whenever I told them I wanted to leave, they said that my egotism was dictating my wishes. My egotism was blinding me: It was not God speaking; it was my selfishness. And, by going against God's will, I was endangering my own eternal salvation. Even when the latter was insinuated and not said explicitly, it had the same effect. The fear of making a mistake and betraying God would freeze my own will. It was hard for me to decipher both: the guilt I felt every time I considered abandoning the movement, and the shame I experienced when I thought of myself as someone "gifted" or valuable. Both feelings—inferiority and superiority in a utilitarian way—would come down like a hammer, banging hard on my soul. Why was being "valuable" enough of a reason to stay?

A vocation to consecrated life depends on God's personal call and the individual's desire to follow, not on the individual's attributes. Even now, I might be a good dancer, but I chose to be a professor, not a dancer. We are the ones who decide, and it is part of God's design. We glorify him by using our own judgment in good faith. We should have recognized RC's utilitarian spirit clearly, but it was given to us in increasing doses, until it became part of our brain process. Now that I have a background on how brain plasticity works and how it "apprehends" patterns and concepts, I see clearly why people who have competent faculties can still be victims.

When we promised never to criticize a superior, we promised it solemnly during a religious ceremony. The promises to live in poverty, chastity, and obedience were said publicly during the liturgy—unless you were under 18, then they would be made in private and those professing had to swear not to tell their parents. But the promise never to criticize superiors, the promise to remain silent before directors' wrongdoings, which we called the "private promise," was made in private before the superior, a Legionary priest, kneeling in front of him... behind closed doors. No one, not even our parents or the bishop, were supposed to know about it. That should have set off an alarm, but how could it? By then, we everything was sorted out in our brains within the "frame" that Maciel was a saint, and RC, God's army. Maciel led us to believe that the Pope had approved all four promises, including the private one. The Pope is venerated in the world and the Pope praised Maciel in our presence numerous times. It was not until after Maciel's death that it became evident that there had never been any such approval.

Ricky, who was now big enough to get on the bed, probably sensed the warmth produced by the heated Florida dream and moved away; he had enough body heat emanating from his hairy body as it was. He jumped and lay down on the cold floor, his stomach facing the ceiling and his legs stretched open, seeking any passing draft. I smiled at the sight of my hippie black pooch. And, once again, I renewed my determination to embrace the second chance life was offering me. My life had become and would continue to be simple.

Looking again at the complacent hairy ball on the floor, I grinned. It was enough to "be" and enjoy the present moment. It was, after all, the only thing within my reach. *Life does not come in a package...but rather, minute by minute.*

I got up.
God, I thank you for this day, I love you, and I need you!
If I have hurt someone, please forgive me.

I prepared coffee. The smell was delicious. How could I have deprived myself of its flavor for years due to acid reflux? While in RC, my heartburn was so severe that there were times when I could hardly move. "It's nerves," some doctors said. "What do they do to you in that place?" an acquaintance of father's, a doctor, had asked me during one of my trips through Houston.

I rushed to put on my yoga outfit. I had agreed to join Rea, a neighbor, at the local yoga joint on East 59th street. After yoga, she and I were planning to create our online dating profiles.

Chapter 9

DARING

"If there is something I learned from my relationships, it's that if you try to fit into a foreign mold, you end up spilling out at the ends," Rea whispered while the yoga instructor was busy adjusting a participant's posture at the front of the room. "What are your non-negotiables in your life? What is it that you must have other than a classroom and some brats to teach?"

Rea was my "new friend," a neighbor from across the hall in the apartment building where I lived my first year in Manhattan. She was from the Ukraine and had a unique way of expressing herself. She would say beautifully constructed sentences, and though she would lose you at the beginning, by the end she always made sense. It was like a harmonious work of art created with splashes of paint.

"I've been out of the order for several months and I still don't know." I quit my yoga pose, placing both hands over my head. "I don't know what I 'need,' but I know what I miss... and I simply got used to missing it during all those years—" the instructor approached us and I hurried to replicate Rea's pose. He still straightened my back and gave me a forced smile. Once he headed back to the front of the room, I whispered: "Of course I miss my family. I also miss my grandfather's ranch in Linares, and my dad's in the Picachos Mountains... the smell of straw, of pines and flowers. I miss the noise of the horses puffing and clashing their horseshoes against the ground... I miss starry nights... I miss the beach... not this beach with freezing water. I miss the southern beach." As I added my last thought, I relinquished my yoga position and sat... visualizing.

"What are you doing in Manhattan, then?" Rea whispered again but this time loudly, and stared at me under her arm in her downward-dog position. "Most likely, the potential husband you'll find here won't miss the things you just described. This is Manhattan!" Apparently, we were too loud. Everyone in the back of the room turned to look at us.

We continued our class in silence.

We got back to our building and I took Ricky to do "potty" on the street. I had finally gotten used to cleaning up after him. It was a strange practice for a "mountain girl."

I was feeling optimistic, healthy, and strong—very different from how I had felt only a few months before. I would never again take my health for granted. I sat on my desk in front of the computer and started to think about my answers while I waited for Rea. Since it was 2002, Perfect Match—the dating site we decided to use—required that we fill out a questionnaire online, submit it as a file, and then visit their headquarters in town to produce a video and pictures, and to pay.

A few minutes later, Rea arrived giggling. Somehow we found "dating online" daring and thrilling. I smiled at the thought that I could think about it with humor.

"Tell us about yourself. How would friends describe you? What are your favorite activities? What do you look for in a relationship?" I read some of the first open-ended questions aloud while she settled in next to me with her laptop.

"You have a rustic inclination," she said without hesitation.

"Of course I am rustic to you. You are 100 percent urban," I said as soon as I registered her comment. She was 35 and had been in Manhattan for 10 years working for one of the banks.

"True—let's just write something and see what comes out," she said.

We worked silently for a while. The task of creating my profile turned out to be one of the best exercises at that point in my life. I was being forced to redefine myself. I wrote the following knowing that I had more questions than answers, and that I would probably erase everything and then rewrite it. "I am from Mexico and I have lived in

Italy, Spain, and the States. I have traveled extensively. I am 37 years old (I was turning 38 that summer) and I was in a Catholic order for 18 years. Teaching is my passion. I don't know what my style of clothes and furniture is yet. I don't have a favorite movie or sport either. I don't know how to apply make-up or do my hair. My favorite activity is to walk barefoot, sleep in a bed, have hot water while I shower, dance while I cook, and eat when I am hungry. Dislikes... I dislike abstinence, eating frozen cans of tuna, waking up when it is still dark, and wearing clothes over my bathing suit on the beach. What do I expect from a relationship? I need someone kind and patient who doesn't mind all the above... with whom I will not feel trapped."

I showed Rea what I had written, and we burst out laughing.

"Wow! It's true... you just want the normal things... That's good, but dangerous... because you could just settle for anyone who is nice, and not right."

I was so happy being alive and healthy that everything was my favorite activity. When I would open my eyes in the morning and feel my brand-new mattress under me, I would smile and thank God from the bottom of my heart—till this day, I do the same. The smile would remain throughout my 10-minute hot shower, and while preparing my own coffee... to my taste, and while I drank it without pain. I could never again take any of that, plus wearing comfortable clothing, being barefoot, and moving my hip to a melody, for granted.

"You can't put that. They're going to think you're a fake...almost, too good to be true."

It did sound too good to be true. I wanted to have sex every day to make up for all those years without it, I wanted to stay healthy and laugh a lot...I didn't need much. Rea was right, I couldn't write that. It was misleading since I still had a sort of dark past.

"You don't even have to say that you were a nun... they will think you're not normal. Even I, knowing you, have a hard time understanding why you joined that place, and how you stayed there for so long." Rea did not know much about my upbringing, my family, Maciel, and the movement. It would still take me several more months before I could explain to her why and how I had joined.

I rewrote my profile several times until it was ready to be published. At the end, I wrote as little as possible. I talked about my career as a teacher, my love for languages, for horses, dogs and nature, and about my positive outlook on life.

I arrived to Perfect Match headquarters the following day after work—Rea was out of town for a few days. I wore jeans, a button down red blouse, a ponytail and little make up... I wanted to look simple. The day before, riding a subway in the early evening—from Grand Central to my school to collect some paper-work—a man dressed in a fancy suit had stopped me to ask if I was interested in working in a gentlemen's club. I was coming back from the gym and was wearing shorts and a tank top. I didn't know what a gentlemen's club was exactly but I imagined it. When I said no, he added that the pay was amazing. I smiled and continued walking. Random people in Manhattan had already described me as Cleopatra, Polynesian Princess, and Aztec goddess. Now, this man had thought I was gentlemen's club material and that added to my insecurity.

When I arrived to Perfect Match looking so plain, a couple of the ladies busied themselves to do my hair and makeup.

During the following weeks, several individuals contacted me through the dating service.

~ ~ ~ ~

I rest over a rock by a river. I am naked and leaning back on my arms... palms over the rock. There is no shame. My face is raised towards the sun, absorbing its rays. A horseman arrives and after dismounting and tying the horse to a tree a few yards from me, he takes his clothes off and submerges under the water. With a hand gesture, he calls me and I follow without hesitation... I know him. Under the water, our bodies join. It is something reverent... like a sacred ritual, and the action, necessary as a means to "know" each other and to merge our hearts at the deepest level.

I woke up. Ricky was sleeping placidly... It was the dog's breathing and not the horseman's that I heard while dreaming. The east sun's bright rays were already piercing the studio.

Yes, I get the hint, I told my subconscious. I need a new outlook on love.

I got up.

God, I thank you for this day, I love you, and I need you!
If I have hurt someone, please forgive me.

I sat at my computer. It had become a routine: at school until the afternoon; in the evening, I had time to prepare lessons, run errands, go to the gym, write emails, and do anything else I wished to do... Weekends or holidays were the same, except that with school not in session, I could work from home. Something people don't realize is that teachers always have homework.

My life was definitively more balanced than what it had been in RC, where I only had three 10-minute breaks a day. The rest of the time, I was in scheduled community activities and tasks. It was the same seven days a week. Sundays and some Thursdays activities would change, but the schedule was tight. "Idleness opens the door to temptations," we were told. During the 10-minute breaks, we had to wash our panties and nylons, sew buttons, clip our nails... Those among us that were able to spend a full 10-minute break in the chapel, praying, received public praises from directors. I was never among them, and always wondered when those women had time to wash their panties, etc. "How can you spare a full 10-minute break in the chapel, when we only have three 10-minute breaks a day?" I asked one of those devoted colleagues once. "It is a matter of getting everything done during the 30 minutes we are given in the morning upon rising," she had explained. Every morning, I attempted to follow her advice, and every morning I failed. I would barely make it on time for morning offering.

Our daily schedule consisted in community prayers and Mass (a total of at least 3 hours), community conversation, housework, study time, time to write letters to members in other communities and once a month to our family. The rest of the time was dedicated to more studies and classes if you were in " formation"—during your first years after consecration—or to " the apostolate"—teaching, preaching, and any other activity that would make RC bigger and stronger.

While the computer rebooted, I glanced at the two-inch crucifix I had on the desk. It was the same crucifix I received when I "got consecrated"—when I promised to live in poverty, chastity and obedience. It was the only object that—in accordance with the movement's rules—I owned.

I had continued to pray since my departure from RC. I prayed every day; however, I could not recite pre-formulated prayers. I even found the liturgy at church painful—a symbol of both: what I missed and what I was beginning to detest.

One of my favorite prayer times was on the subway. It was there that I had time to do a contemplative prayer: become aware of my surroundings and my present moment, and then contemplate God's love towards everyone around me; to make an act of love for them and the creator who made them, and an act of faith that their lives would be meaningful and that they would find joy and fulfillment. It was an opportunity to foster empathy for those riding next to me... to join them in their prayers, joys, and sufferings. Sometimes I would listen to Taizé music and repeat the verses in my head... "You are eternally wonderful, oh Lord." I am grateful to RC and to the Holy Spirit for teaching me to meditate. Thanks to the thousands of hours reading about contemplative meditation, prayer became my cornerstone and the only thing that kept me sane. I learned that a good book can be a lifeline—had it not been for my reading of spiritual masters such as Augustine or Tomas Aquinas, I would have lost my faith in the Church altogether. Instead, I learned to take the Catholic Church at face value: The Church was Christ, but Christ was not the Church. To say that Christ was the Church meant putting limits to God. God might be the Church in the same way He contains everything, but He is also greater than the Church.

I received several automated emails to my phone during the day; there were some messages or "requests" waiting for me at Perfect Match. And as I logged in that morning, I saw portraits of men I did not know; each had a note on the side. I skimmed through all six pictures and their messages quickly. One of them caught my attention, Jack from Manhattan. He seemed to be about 40. I couldn't tell what color his eyes were since both his mouth and eyes were grinning. He appeared kind and sweet. He had a well-defined jaw-line covered by three or four days of stubble... dark as the disheveled mop of hair on his head. He was not handsome—or was he? It probably didn't matter. I was looking for respect and affection—a type of maturity and tenderness that would facilitate trust and intimacy. I needed someone who would understand me and help me reinvent myself without dominating me, without controlling my likes, my mind and conscience. My most recent long-term point of reference was RC, where I had developed feelings of insecurity, and guilt for craving legitimate friendship, where even hugs and kisses on the cheek had been deemed "inappropriate." My reference was also Fr. Maciel and his patriarchate, where women were told how to walk, stand, sit, eat and, even, how to position our hands and arms when kneeling during prayers. A professional career "in the world" could demand a certain type of behavior, but nothing like what we experienced. The control was detailed, strict, and 24/7. One day, a community supervisor called me to her office.

"Please stand in front of me with your hands loose but together in front of you... like this." She stood and placed her hands one palm over the back of the other hand, in front of her abdomen. "What does this look like?"

I observed guardedly for a few seconds looking at the woman's body and posture. Puzzled, I gazed back at her eyes. "I am not sure if I understand... What does what look like?"

With a sigh, the woman said, not frustrated but with a tone of solemnity: "You are calling too much attention to 'that' part of the body by standing the way you usually do," the word "that" said emphatically as the woman opened her eyes widely. She was referring to my crotch.

I understood and thanked her for the observation before asking for permission to be excused. I made sure to keep a smile until I left her office... not a smirk, not a grin, not an incredulous look, just a humble and grateful smile, otherwise she would probably accuse me of not accepting God's will unconditionally. I kept walking in shock. It has been over 15 years since the incident and—till this day—every time I stand, I do not know what to do with my hands... God forbid I "draw attention to 'that' part." I was trained to believed everything "God's representatives" told me.

My mind was back to "Jack from Manhattan." I clicked on his profile, and there he was: Jack with no last name. He was 45, divorced with two kids, and was an AIG (American International Group) high-ranking official. I didn't know what AIG was at the time. Also, having been born in a family of successful entrepreneurs, business ranks did not have an effect on me, as I noticed they had on Rea and my new Manhattan acquaintances; I simply took them for granted... maybe too much.

I read Jack's profile carefully, reading in between the lines. *Was he too structured? Would he feel he owned me because he had much more to offer than me?*

Jack described himself as good-humored, and with good stamina. I had a better view of his arms now. He seemed strong. I looked into his hazel smiley eyes. I liked what I saw. He was not handsome. *Good!* I had developed phobia to competition.

I smiled back at him and clicked to accept.

I woke up at 6 a.m.—as usual—the following day.
God, I thank you for this day, I love you, and I need you.
If I have hurt someone, please forgive me.

I noticed a red light on my phone. I had a message from Jack. I felt butterflies. I pictured him sitting at his computer with his attractive arms over the desk while his hands typed, his hazel eyes reflecting the screen's brightness. "Hello—Thanks for your note. I've never done this and I don't know where to start. Would it be easier to speak on the phone? Let me know. I'll be at work until 6 pm. We can speak after that if you wish. Here is my phone number." The dating site I was using had a background check system to verify that all of the profiles were authentic and no one had a criminal record.

I noticed that his phone number's area code was from New Jersey. I had memorized most of the USA area codes at the time, a perk from my work at RC.

For a moment I wished he were from a place in the woods among hills and horses, where he could take me and we could live happily ever after. Instead of sharing my secret desires with him, I wrote: "Sure! Are you from New Jersey? I grew up by the mountains, I love animals and I have 3 brothers and 3 sisters :-)... How is it where you grew up? Do you like Manhattan? I am thinking about moving to the suburbs to be close to the City but surrounded by the countryside... killing two birds with one stone (per se... I don't kill birds... my father is both an ornithologist and an ecologist). Do you want to chat tonight?"

I reread my note, and I erased it. Instead, I wrote "Sure. I will call at around 7 pm. Looking forward." And even then, before pressing send, I stopped to think what would Rea say about the note? Would she think it is too much information... or not enough? I decided I could not make the mistake of depending on others' decisions again, and I pressed send. *If I scare Jack... let it be!* There would be others, and I had to start somewhere.

"What brought you to New York?" Jack asked shortly after we started our phone conversation that evening.

"It's a long story." *How much to say?* Speaking to him had turned out to be harder than what I had expected. "Did you read my profile?"

"Yes... but you don't say much about your life before New York."

"Oh, yes... I was... a nun." *Or almost a nun, or more than a nun...*

There was a moment of silence. He was probably digesting the shock. I wasn't sure if he would find it romantic as in *The Sound of Music*... or terrifying as in the horror movie, *The Nun*.

"Oh... like in a religious order?"

"Yes." When the topic of my "religious life" would come up in a conversation, I noticed people would be either overly enthused or too quiet.

"How interesting; for how long?"

My throat was dry and I needed to swallow. *Interesting*, I had learned, was the response given as an alternative polite option for "strange."

"From 19 to 37... How about you?"

"What about me?" he said.

"Were you in an order before working for AIG?"

He laughed. I felt immediately relieved. *Ask questions so they don't ask you; besides, who doesn't want to talk about themselves.*

"So you don't have a lot of experience with men, I presume," he said.

"No."

"Well… neither do I."

We laughed again.

Jack and I went out several times. He appeared to have everything I thought I was looking for, except that he was not interested in remarrying—*been there, done that* kind of attitude.

I asked him once, before his company car dropped me off at my building, if he would consider getting a marriage annulment and marrying in the Catholic Church. At that point in my life, it was the only "right path" I knew.

"Maybe I can come up and we can talk about it," he said.

I found no objection to it this since it was early.

80

Chapter 10

Friends

When we first walked into my apartment, we kissed in the foyer, and we kissed again on the sofa... In Jack's language, and the language of most people, that meant we would probably make love and stay in bed for the rest of the evening... maybe get something to eat at midnight. But in my language, it was a new "word" that I had not deciphered before that moment... and as I understood, I broke away from the kiss, the embrace, and the rest that was happening. I quickly stood up next to the sofa where Jack remained in awe. I uncoiled my skirt, buttoned my blouse, and with my shaky fingers combed my messy hair. He stayed there with his eyes closed, and his elbows on his knees... his fingers later brushed his hair back and he let out a frustrated sigh. Without saying a word, I went to the refrigerator and offered him something to eat. Strangely, I thought of an aunt who used to fix all awkward moments with food. And so, without waiting for an answer, I started to prepare a sandwich.

Considering Jack's background, I see now how patient he was with me.

"Can I ask you something personal... that might not be conventional?" I asked him. We were back at my apartment, one Saturday afternoon, weeks after the almost-made-love scene.

"If you are going to ask me to marry you... I inform you that it is not considered 'unconventional' any more for the woman to be the one who asks."

"Funny," I said. I was now able to recognize and understand almost all of his jokes.

"Thanks."

"We have known each other for almost two months. But I don't know a lot about you. For example, would you mind telling me about your marriage?"

He looked at me: "So, what would you like to know about my marriage?" His voice showed a certain stress.

"Well... for example, what kind of relationship did you have with your ex-wife?"

He got up from the sofa and went to the kitchen to get some coffee. My studio apartment was all one big open space so I watched him in the process.

"Never mind," I said.

He paused and then said: "Don't do that." His voice was calm. He sat back next to me again.

"Do what?"

"You're retreating, to the place where you go when you're being insecure, afraid of being vulnerable. You, more than anyone, should trust your instincts."

"It was just a bad question?" I could hear the frustration in my voice.

"There's nothing wrong with asking when you need to know an answer. I'm no expert, but it might even be the first step in intimacy. You repressed your questions too long." He finally breathed in. "You asked a question that's important to you... Please hear my answer... I just needed time to think about how to say it... I wasn't making up a lie or a way to avoid the question... I'm not Maciel or RC."

I had told Jack as much as possible about my experience in RC, though it had been hard because I could not see—exactly—what were the movement's flaws. I could only see my flaws, and why I couldn't stay. Jack, on the other hand, had done his own research and seemed to understand, better than me, about my fears.

Wow! *Where were you during the last 15 years of my life?* I needed that so badly. All relationships should be able to ruffle some feathers if that brings them to deeper trust and intimacy, I thought. I had never experienced that in my adulthood. I looked at him—into his eyes—and waited.

"I'll start by saying that I feel extremely embarrassed about what I'm going to say," he continued. The sounds of cars in the street below us became acute to my senses.

"I was unfaithful. I had a relationship with one of the secretaries in the office for a few months. It was stupid and I regretted it. However, my wife found out about it and forbade me to come back into the house. We have two young children, as you know, so it killed me... But it was too late."

I was shocked.

He paused and looked back at me. "So, how was my marriage? It was wonderful, until it was no longer." He smiled but his smile did not reach his eyes... nor did it erase his frown. "At the end, it was hell. Once the trust was broken, there was nothing I could do. She didn't want me back. I begged her to try again, especially after we found out that our son was diabetic. But she said we could parent the kids and care for them without being together. And, just like that, we became part of the 50-percent divorce rate statistics."

"Why did you do it?" Tears were trickling down my face. Maciel was, in my opinion, perverse... an evil megalomaniac... and an abusive narcissist. Jack was not.

"Stupid male ego," he responded as he exhaled. "She gave me what, at that point, I was not getting from my wife." There was a pause; then he held me by my arms. "You lived a perfectly chaste life for 18 years... This must sound inexplicable, right?"

Did it? Not really. "No... and I can't judge you," I said. "We all make decisions based on who we are in the moment of the decision..." I added, and I meant it. It was something I told myself every time I questioned my past "stupidities" and my bad decisions. It had become clearer to me that life was not a cycle but rather a spiral... since we can rectify our steps, even retrace them, but never erase them... That is why it makes more sense, I had concluded, to go through life slowly, rather than fast. "Would you act differently now?" I asked hopefully.

"Yes." It was a timid but sincere statement.

"Who is she?" *Had I said that aloud?*

"One of the assistants at the office. She is a Kama Sutra trainer," he added as he raised his eyebrows. "You met her at the Christmas party."

Of course I remembered her... She was gorgeous... "Is she still at AIG?" I managed to ask.

"Yes," he replied as he closed the distance between us. "At a different office now."

That night, before going to bed, I researched *Kama Sutra*. My eyes quickly skimmed the Wikipedia page... I read: "Aims and priorities in life... the union of the physical and spiritual affection, communicating through the embrace..." Then... *Oh, my...* "Types of embraces, caressing, how to help the woman relax" and more... I had a feeling a good Theology of the Body session could substitute the Kama Sutra Manual, but then... what did I know?

Jack's infidelity scared me. With my trust issues and insecurities, I wasn't sure I could learn to trust him. There had been a time, while I was in RC, when a superior arrived to the Rhode Island center, and asked us to gather in the conference room for an important announcement. And just like that, with no preamble, no explanation, he announced someone else would take my place. He did not take the time to speak to me, and explain. He simply said in public: "She is a holy, kind, and brilliant woman, and she will be responsible for all the apostolate in North America." I had been trained to smile and thank God for the opportunity to be humble... not humiliated... and accept that someone else had arrived to do my work. I could handle my feelings of sadness; they were after all, just that—a feeling... For sure, after the conference, he would approach me and tell me how my services were needed elsewhere. But no... no one had approached me that day, or the following... nor that week, or the following. No one offered an explanation or provided an assignment. That detail was "secondary," since "someone docile had arrived," my superior had finally explained to me. "Since you are so good at starting from zero, you are going to California..." The fading voice had continued talking about opening a school there... maybe a university... Yeah! Things in the East Coast and Midwest had expanded and my lack of blind obedience had become an issue... I could mislead others... Oh... and it was a perfect lesson of humility: "You see Elena... we all are... you are 100 percent replaceable... the needs of the Kingdom are priority," the director explained.

I am well aware now that this happens in the workplace. The reason why it is so devastating when it happens in a sect is that the group has taken the role of your family. What that superior did to me that day was emotionally insensitive and extremely harmful, but I did not have the assertiveness and courage to mention it. That experience ratified a sentiment of shame and unworthiness... I accepted the humiliation I did not deserve, and I concluded that RC could not be my family. My family would never discard me like that... and if it did, it didn't deserve to be my family. That "incident" was the weight that made the balance incline towards the option of leaving.

I never got over the fear that Jack would cheat on me, but I never told him about it. I feared I was being unreasonable. Fear, just like in RC, paralyzed me.

After Jack and I broke up the two-month relationship, I quit the dating service and—instead—I met some casual friends. Robert was from the suburbs, and I met him through a former boarding school roommate. He had sold his business for several million, and was still working as an executive in Stamford, not far from the city. He was a widower and had three teenage kids. He was sweet and mature, and maybe was right for me but, somehow, I felt I wouldn't keep up with the social demands of the town where he lived. I was afraid to fail again. I was pretty sure that, within me, there was a free-spirited woman that eventually would find her way out of her stoic shell. Luke, on the other hand, lived a totally spontaneous life and went, every day, where his "inspiration" would lead...with no social commitments. He could do it because the dogs he walked for others, to keep busy during the day, couldn't complain. That's how we had met, walking our dogs. He could afford a large apartment a few blocks from the UN, in Manhattan, since he had inherited it together with a substantial trust, which paid for taxes and all of his jetsetter expenses. With what he made walking dogs, he paid for his gym membership. "I need to be in shape to hold those leashes," he explained to me once. I found it fascinating: he worked as a dog-walker to pay for the gym, and went to the gym to be able to walk the dogs. I believe he simply enjoyed both. He was in search of a "female companion"—never used the word "wife"— who would share his love for animals, especially dogs. There was no mention of children either. There was also a man who had just left the consecrated life in Opus Dei, a Catholic group similar to RC. He had approached me one day when I stopped at St. Agnes Church, by Grand Central, to pray... He worked in finances. He was a good choice but "too good to be true." The irony is that he probably thought the same about me because we had been trained for years to be perfect. He concluded he probably needed time to adjust just like I did. Finally, there was William, two years younger than me, and a friend of one of my acquaintances at the UN—where I had done my internship. He was kind, handsome, Catholic, and had never been married.

 I didn't know if I felt "chemistry" with any of them, but then, I wasn't sure I knew how chemistry felt.

 There were a few things I should have learned at that point, but they did not sink in until after an extremely painful relationship that lasted over 10 years. One of them was the discovery—through one of the dating-site personality tests—that there is a side of me that loves order; I am a planner (short, medium, and long-term planner); but there is, as well, an equally strong side that is creative and spontaneous. I have actually spent many hours painting, writing, and performing dances since I left the movement... especially in these past few years... activities that—with no doubt—bring me to my happy place. Most humans have both sides and it is up to each of us to determine what is the perfect combination of planning and spontaneity we need to be happy. In my case, even though I find planning to be extremely necessary and therapeutic, when it is done with no spontaneous and creative outlet, it takes a toll on me. Letting my partner rely on me for all organization and planning—while he was the fun and spontaneous parent—did not work for me because I found myself hating the person I became, the same person I had been in RC.

I believe people quit a lifestyle, or get divorced not because the "love dries out," or due to some "attribute" that makes the other person unlovable, but rather because they hate the person they become... and they cannot live with themselves. That is why they escape.

I was going to see William that night, and could not decide what to wear. Ricky had ripped apart a fashion magazine I purchased the day before at the grocery store. I actually had hoped to learn to dress a bit more fashionably. In RC, I was given six outfits that I could wear. The director or someone of her choice would buy and assign the clothes. In a way, it was easier when I did not have to choose... On the other hand, I considered the clothes ugly... Once, during a pilgrimage to the Shrine of Our Lady of Lourdes, in France, I overheard a man warning his traveling companion about a group of gypsies approaching... When I looked at the group of so-called gypsies, I realized it was a group of my RC colleagues! And as I observed, I concluded that indeed, we could pass for a group of homeless gypsies. It was cold and many were wearing wool scarves over their heads. I was horrified. So much for "good appearance" as one of the requirements to join RC. Why would Maciel only accept "decently" looking women—as he would say, indicating that the women we recruited ought to be good looking—if then, they had to dress like that?

After my brief fashion research, I was relieved to find out that jeans and a t-shirt or a pullover sweater could still be fashionable. The only thing that seemingly changed every two to three years was how tight or loose one was supposed to wear them. Now the t-shirts were back to being tight. I opted for jeans and t-shirt and prayed I wouldn't be underdressed. William dressed very well.

"Let's go Ricky! We need fresh air... otherwise I will start chewing things like you do." I could feel the tension in my body. "Did you see what just happened? I tried on my whole wardrobe," I shared with the pooch. My furry friend stared back at me through his bangs and sat still... after tilting his head sideway, he raised his ears. Shih-tzu dogs had been bred at the emperors' house in China to be companions. Ricky was a good listener; after all, he was genetically wired for that.

~ ~ ~ ~

My students are waiting for me in the classroom. Immaculate College is RC's university and "novitiate" for women. I was supposed to be teaching the Anthropology class that summer—like I did every summer—to about 30 women. I see myself entering the room wearing, besides a pair of black high-heel strappy sandals, nothing but a lace bra and panties, also black. And as I walk in, I advance slowly towards the front of the room, then... uncoiling my upper body, I lean back on the professor's desk... palms on the oversized dark wood surface supporting my body, and one heel casually resting over the other. I start the lesson. "The feeling of security is a very important consideration in the study of Anthropology." I am pacing across the front of the room resembling more a Victoria Secret runway model than a college professor... or consecrated virgin. My hips push forward and rock as I carry on with long strides. "Anthropology..." I hear myself saying as I skim the room, "studies the human person and, therefore, allows for the privileged opportunity to reflect on what self-esteem and security mean to us, women consecrated to God. What we wear under our clothes can help us feel beautiful. In philosophy, we call it a perfect syllogism," I stop and look at my audience. Everyone is motionless. I place my hands on my hips and keep my feet apart. "You will feel beautiful if you are beautiful, and tell me: who wouldn't feel beautiful wearing a lace bra and panties like these? Then, of course, you have to match the colors to your skin. Some skin tones look better with pink or sky-blue. For example, considering my tanned skin, I look better wearing black, white, red, sapphire-blue, and emerald-green. Anthropological studies have demonstrated that women who feel beautiful will be considered beautiful... if not by everyone, then by almost everyone. Therefore, we will ask Father Maciel to establish a new rule in RC: no more cotton panties. Lace and only lace... like this one." I conclude my lecture, opening my arms and slowly turning on my heel,s allowing the students to appreciate the clothing details. And while I am still turning, Father Maciel walks into the room. He shows a noticeable erection under his black trousers, which starts to grow. And in one instant it grows so much, still covered by his equally growing pants and jacket, that stretching out to the ceiling's chandelier, it knocks it down!

    I did not stay to see the damage done to the chandelier's crystal as it smashed on the floor. I woke up.

    Another crazy dream... I had just purchased some "pretty" bras and panties—all lace. I had followed the recommendation of a stranger given to another stranger in the gym's dressing rooms. The woman had explained to her friend that it was important to wear "pretty" undergarments "even when only you get to see them. You will feel attractive, and if you feel attractive, you will act attractive. Women who act attractive, present themselves as attractive," the stranger had explained. At the moment I simply reflected on the fact that she had quoted what we would call in philosophy, a syllogism: If A, equals B, and B equals C, then A equals C. Apparently, the idea had crawled up into my sub-conscience and had taken rest there. When I woke up, I couldn't stop laughing. My subconsciousness was finding the humor in my past life. Maybe it was a way to heal. There was hope for me after all.

God, I thank you for my life, I love you, and I need you.
If I have hurt someone, please forgive me.

Chapter 11

IDENTITY

It was snowing the morning William and I flew from New York to Monterrey. It was November of 2002, and we had been dating for a few months. I felt better then, than a year before, when I visited for Christmas right after I had left RC. Now I was bringing my future husband—Catholic and unmarried, bright and handsome as a bonus. It was a success story. By then, I also had a Lucy—a honey-white female Shih-tzu; and, both—Ricky and Lucy—flew to Monterrey with us.

As I contemplated the beautiful Monterrey mountain ranges, getting taller and more majestic as we approached the city, I could not be still. Rules in RC stipulated that members could visit home every seven years; unless you were in the same country where parents or siblings resided, then you could see them for a weekend once a year... But you would still have to spend the night in the RC center—if there was one in town—and the curfew was 6 p.m. You had to arrive to the center for community prayers and dinner. Therefore, during my 18 years in the movement, I had visited home only twice. I had known that, since my father was RC benefactor, I probably could have gotten permission to visit them more often, especially after the first seven years... when I was a bit more "settled" in my vocation, according to superiors.... "God forbid she runs back to her ex-boyfriend's arms and abandons the movement...." as RC leaders used to fear when I first entered. And since I did not want to enjoy the privileges of coming from a wealthy family, my parents and siblings had been the ones to travel to see me as often as they could... Still, it was probably not fair to those coming from little money... but how could the movement prevent parents from visiting their daughters once a year?

Years later we found out Maciel fathered two sons and one daughter with two different women. He had even visited an RC center with the second woman and their daughter. He was seen traveling with them numerous times and they were always introduced as the wife and daughter of a Legionary benefactor. Maciel spent weeks at a time enjoying family life and the luxuries the order's money allowed them. No wonder the money collected from schools, both tuitions and donations, would go up like smoke! The irony. He stole money right under people's noses. In addition to his monthly allowance of $25,000 for unforeseen needs—half of the annual median income in the USA—he constantly requested funds. No one ever asked him for an expense report. On the other hand, he would demand detailed reports from us. He probably thought us capable of stealing—it takes one to know one. The vow of silence and the cult-to-self protected him; semi-gods are untouchable.

I skimmed the landscape. During my vocational recruitment trips in the USA, I traveled by car across most of the States. Monterrey's rocky mountains reminded me of those in Colorado. I did those trips even during the coldest winters. Sometimes our cans of food, kept in the trunk of the car, would freeze and we would eat tuna ice-pops for days. Our weekly budget was barely enough for gas and food. I had felt so poor, so faithful to the Gospel. Now I know I overdid it. I shouldn't have led my body to anemia. No one should have to surrender one's own judgment. I was finally doing something for myself and by myself... I had chosen William, the one I thought my family would approve. I prayed I had chosen the right man. Even then, flying to Monterrey so he could meet my family, I doubted myself. Maybe I was dreaming it all. Everything seemed distant, as if I was living someone else's life. I had told no one at work about my past. With them, I was Elena, a Mexican-American immigrant and southerner, working in East Harlem with a low to medium income. In Monterrey, I remained as Andres and Pilar's fifth child, the daughter of a well-known ecologist, a philanthropic and successful business man... and a religious, energetic, and loving woman who was deeply involved in her community. I was the daughter who had joined RC as a teen. And, in RC, I was the "ambassador" of everything the movement represented—or was supposed to represent—in the USA, Canada, Australia, and New Zealand... Oddly, one world did not know the Elena who belonged to the other two. I don't know how it happened. Maybe I was not all that different from Maciel—the man who lived a double life. The thought disgusted me. Which of the three "Elenas" would marry William? I tried to place my mind and emotions in the right frame before arriving... My family needed to see I was ready for marriage.

Part II

Vindicating—Yet Horrific—Truth

Chapter 12

MACIEL

In 2005, two years after my wedding, and a month after John Paul II's death, Cardinal Ratzinger (later elected as Pope Benedict XVI), ordered an investigation against Maciel. The 1997 and 1998 accusations—made public by Hartford Currant journalist Jason Berry, and presented to Ratzinger as head of the Congregation of the Faith—became pivotal in the investigation. A year later, in 2006, the Congregation's investigator presented Benedict XVI with a report declaring Maciel guilty of sex abuse and theft. Though the Vatican did not make the evidence collected in the investigation public—and did not even share them with the Legion and RC's officials—the witnesses did. I do not know any of the witnesses that came forward, yet again, in 1997 and 1998, but I do recall the following three stories of victims whose real names I omitted.

Peter, a First Witness - 1958

It had been two years since Peter Joseph Olivos had solemnly sworn to "tell the truth, and nothing but the truth" as he raised his right hand before a crucifix. The Vatican's investigator, had asked only one question, "Did Father Maciel ever do something inappropriate or illicit, and ask you not to tell anyone, not even during confession?" Peter's reply had been simple and somewhat abrupt, "No."

The Vatican had been investigating accusations made against Maciel, and he was temporarily suspended from his duties as Director of the Legion of Christ.

Peter should have felt proud for having been loyal to *Nuestro Padre;* but, that night, the day he lied, he had not slept well. He had sleepless nights for two consecutive years. Technically, he deserved to be excommunicated from the Church for having lied in such an interview.

Brother Peter was the Dean of Discipline in one of the Legion's all boys' schools in Mexico City. He was observing Alma through his office window. Alma was a third grade teacher; she was new and was struggling with two of her students. Who could blame her? She was a small-town girl from Morelia and many of the students attending the school were wealthy, arrogant, and spoiled. Despite Alma's dedication and encouragement, two of them were making her life impossible.

Peter realized Alma was gazing back at him from the school's playground, smiling. How long had he been staring at her, lost in his thoughts about Maciel, about her difficult student... and about her? Peter smiled back and sat at his desk. He would target the next pending issue.

The door to his office opened and Alma's young and smiley face popped in, "Can I come in, Brother?"

"Of course," Peter heard himself saying enthusiastically. "How are things with the two Musketeers?" he asked to divert the attention away for the tone of his voice.

"A bit better, thank you. I would like to speak to you about something else... something personal... Brother." She was supposed to call Peter, Brother Peter. Since he was not ordained yet, he was not Father Peter.

"Sit down, please," he replied.

"I know you seminarians are reserved, but... you seem awfully sad. Is there something we can do?" Alma's brother had left the seminary a few months back due to depression and she had become especially sensitive to sad seminarians.

Peter and Alma had become friends during his years as Dean... maybe more than what the rules allowed. "I'm not what I appear to be, Alma; there is something I need to tell you and it might change the way you feel about me." Peter needed to talk to someone and it seemed that the moment to do so had finally arrived. He turned to face the window again and looking at the clouds condensing as the wind pushed them around, he said, "I had a homosexual relationship."

"Was it with a minor or with an adult?" There was no judgment in Alma's tone of voice. She was worried.

"Adult... it was a priest," Peter replied quickly. He imagined that would relieve Alma... and he was right. It was one thing to choose to have a sexual relationship, and it was very different to abuse a minor... especially a student.

"How old were you?"

"Sixteen."

"Peter," Alma said, "please... turn around and look at me."

Peter turned and saw her... very close to him. She kissed him... and Peter responded to the kiss, which was followed by an embrace.

"I don't believe I'm homosexual... in case that's what you're wondering," Peter said.

The young teacher sat again on the chair opposite to the desk as if nothing had happened. "What are you going to do?" Alma asked.

"I don't know... I think I lost my capacity to judge years back."

"I will give you the phone number of a person who can help you," she said as she took a blank piece of paper from the desk, "This is the doctor that helped my brother when he was trying to discern. He lives here in Mexico City. He will understand..." Alma fixed her gaze on Peter as she handed him the note and said, "Peter, please... promise me you'll call him."

Peter wrote to Fr. Maciel the same afternoon he met with Dr. Martinez. He asked for dispensation of his vows in the Legion: "I believe I need to leave and seek professional mental health," he wrote.

When Maciel received Peter's letter, he replied with a telephone call. He wanted no record of what he wished to say. "You can leave immediately. And when you get one of those stupid jobs outside, you can start paying the Legion for your studies." He had appraised them at about $40,000. "I always feared you were a bad investment, Peter. What a pity... and I was right: a waste of resources." Maciel concluded the conversation by saying, "You are weak." Peter had followed Dr. Martinez advice, "Play the game, Peter. The narcissist has an acute sense of what he perceives to be *his rights*. He thinks everything is owed to him. His expectations are generally irrational. In his made-up world, you are the aggressor and he is the victim. Simply accept his wishes, terms, and conditions... he cannot harm you anymore, because you are not letting him subdue you... you are just playing a role, in order to outsmart a very smart vicious man."

Peter had been lucky. Not all seminarians who had administered "medical relief" to Maciel during his sexual rituals would find an Alma and a Dr. Martinez.

Years later, two former Legion seminarians wanted to know if he would publicly testify against Maciel. Peter testified, not for himself, but for his grandchildren and the grandchildren of many others.

Fabio, a Second Witness - 1962

It had been over three years since Pius XII's death. Maciel had been reestablished as the Legion's General Director. The Vatican's investigators were unable to gather evidence that would back up the accusations of drug addiction and sexual abuse presented by some clergy and former members. Seemingly, it had all been the result of a confabulation against him, motivated by envy, and encouraged by a group of communists and Church enemies. That was the explanation Maciel offered upon his return to his communities, after over two years of exile.

Fabio Guzman listened to Maciel intently. He had heard it many times in different countries. He had traveled with Maciel to bring the good news of his re-installment to the communities around the word— by that time, the order had expanded to Mexico, Spain, Italy, and Ireland.

"I don't understand the Council Fathers," Maciel said, with a gesture of displeasure referring to the Catholic leaders—all of them Cardinals—gathered at that point in Rome to agree on Church reforms. "Some of them want to allow Catholic priests to marry... Can you imagine? Married priests! There is no way I could touch a woman and later celebrate Mass."

Fabio looked at him incredulously, and Maciel corresponded with a wink of an eye. Fabio then turned to look at Brother Ruben. Ruben avoided eye contact.

Less than 24 hours ago, Fabio and Ruben had been with Maciel in the room of an inn in the South of Ireland. The three had an austere Irish dinner, and an entertaining and pleasant conversation with the hotel owner, who was half Irish and half Scottish and had a lot to say about everything. Maciel, Fabio, and Ruben had then gone back to their rooms. Then, after telling both young men to join him in his room, Maciel lay down. Without asking, Ruben knew exactly what to do. He immediately prepared the priest's injection... five years providing the service trained him to anticipate the priest's drug needs. Maciel removed his clothes and asked Fabio to give him the habitual "massage."

"Ruben..." Maciel said slowly, "Fabio just doesn't get it. Can you please show him how to do it so the massage can produce its effect?"

Fabio should be used to the massages by now... He had been "assisting" Maciel since he was 12; and Maciel constantly instructed him on how to do the job. Seemingly, there were variables to consider depending on the situation and Maciel's health. But in all those years, the founder had been the only one who touched him. Yet, this time, he was asked to remove his clothes for Ruben.

After that trip, Fabio refused to "comply" and he was sent to serve in the missions of Chetumal, a jungle in Mexico. He knew his ordination would be placed on hold indefinitely. He remained in Chetumal for seven years, at the end of which, he was up for a family visit. And when he walked into the rectory of his hometown's Church, he fell to the floor: "Forgive me Father, for I have sinned."

Ruben, a Third Witness - 1976

Ruben wrote to Maciel, in the hope that he would accept his crimes and repent. "When I wrote to you 10 years ago, I asked you to explain to me why you lived such a contradictory life. I never received an answer; instead, two weeks later, I was transferred to the minor seminary in Spain, and my priestly ordination was postponed for years. It is not only you who have proof of your crimes. You might have the homosexual child pornography you crafted to make it appear as if we were coming on to you. I never told you I had some proof of my own, taken when you invited me to your orgies. In the pictures I took, my dear Father, you appear clearly to be the aggressor, fondling two 13-year-olds. You treated us like sex slaves. Will Church officials accept your bribe and sell their souls considering there is such a reliable piece of evidence? This is my last plea, Father. If you do not repent and change your ways, I will send copies of my evidence to Vatican officials."

In the letter, Ruben mentioned two names of priests I had met who had suffered from dementia: "Did you think I would go crazy like Fathers Boa and Saraviego... a convenient way to dismiss my accusations? How can a mentally ill person be a reliable witness, right? I, myself, thought I would go crazy many times, but God has allowed me to remain psychologically hurt, but coherent."

Then he stated something I had noticed in RC—it was a damage control system that Maciel mastered. "You would control the damage by making up one or two lies against us: 'I caught them in homosexual behavior... What a horror. They promised they would not do it again but if there is an abnormality in their behavior or comments, please just let me know,'" you warned my supervisors after each abuse.

Finally, Ruben answered the question some of us had asked—*Does Maciel suffer a double personality disorder?* He wrote: "Once, when I confronted you, you assured me that you were not aware of your behavior. You faked some kind of double personality; on the other hand, you were very well aware of everything... I could tell by the way you would cover up your drunkenness and your drugs."

"You should know that when you transferred me to the minor seminary in Spain, punished for not wanting to bring children to your room any longer... Father Gilberto and others that, like me, had been punished and sent away, continued with the orgies." I had known Father Gilberto well. I knew many young men who had been to weekend retreats with him. I couldn't believe what I was reading.

Ruben then referred to the money used in the trips and the nights at the Waldorf Astoria with expensive cognac for room service.

And what came next was just as disturbing. "How do you think I feel when I hear my sister has been on a weekend retreat with one of the priests you "trained" as an abuser, a priest I have seen with my own eyes having sexual relations with you? What do you think I conclude when I hear my cousin—who is overweight and has dark skin—is not invited to the retreat to which my sister, who is beautiful, was invited? Why do you dismiss the fact that my cousin has better grades and manifests a true inclination towards religious life?"

I understood what Ruben said. In several occasions, I had been asked to send women home just because their appearance was not favorable! "With the men is different," I was told, "They will be priests, that grants them an automatic leadership...But women in RC ought to be OK looking or better; it is our charism." How much had I struggled to accept that practice; at that point, I did not see the connection with Maciel's narcissism.

Ruben also wrote about "the inhumane conditions" in which Maciel had the consecrated women living at the Center in Dublin. He finished by saying that if he—or anyone –approached his sister again, inviting her to a retreat or the consecrated life, he would release the information and the pictures he kept to the authorities at the Vatican.

As it turns out, Ruben's sister was invited to RC recruiting-events and Ruben gave the letter and the proofs to the Vatican's nuncio in the States, who personally delivered them to the Congregation of Religious at the Vatican… the "department"—at that point—in charge of priests' misconduct.

When I read the letter, my mind was spinning, making connections in my head: the letter was sent to Maciel in 1978, and one year after the nuncio informed Vatican Officials of Maciel's unlawful acts, in 1979, Ratzinger, the future Pope, received it. But John Paul II still saw the accusations against Maciel as nothing but calumnies and invited the founder of the "most powerful order in the world—the Legion and RC," to accompany him on his visit to Mexico in a historical trip where both appeared as heroes. My parents had attended the Mass with both the Pope and Maciel during that trip. That same year, he impregnated one of his steady mistresses, using his pseudo name of Maciel Rivero.

Ruben left the priesthood in 1990, the same year I attended an audience with John Paul II, at the Vatican, in which he told me… looking straight into my eyes: "I love Father Maciel."

Chapter 13

FIRST RC YOUTH AND FAMILY ENCOUNTER

I wish I had known the stories of the dozens of Peters, Fabios, and Rubens who were true blackbirding victims. But then, I did know of them, and I believed Maciel when he said they were troubled men, used by the devil to bring the Church down.

I, unfortunately, helped mitigate the effects of their testimonies recounted in Berry's 1997 Hartford Courant's article. In February of 1996, I was assigned with the task to organize the first RC Youth and Family Encounter—a gathering where thousands of members could come together to meet Father Maciel and learn more about him. The Territorial Director told me "it should be about the Founder." The activities should lead participants to get to know and love Father Maciel. He said that it would help RC members—and members to be—to love their vocation in RC, which translated into loving their vocation in the Church. He even insinuated that it should be a grand event, with wide media access since it should alleviate the potential damage brought about by the testimonies of a few madmen, who were going to speak ill of our founder.

A few weeks before the Encounter, while Father Maciel visited our center in Rhode Island, he said I should invite my parents, especially my father, for whom I needed to pray because "his weak faith sometimes doesn't let him sympathize with RC's ways." Indeed, my father supported my mother's work in RC, but never fully sympathized with the order. Maciel knew it, and talked about his brilliant mind as a "lack of faith." It was a perfect way to undermine his potential negativity towards the order.

Over 3,000 people gathered at the Encounter. They came from almost every state to hear Maciel speak and pray. I was asked to give one of the conferences. The title of my talk was "This Is Our Founder." For 40 minutes I praised the presumed character of a man who turned out to be an abusive narcissist, thief, and serial rapist.

When the Legionary territorial director told us we needed to *promote* Nuestro Padre to counteract what his enemies would try to do, we didn't even ask ourselves why he had enemies. We had been taught to believe that saints in the Church have enemies out of jealousy, or simply because the devil wants to weaken the Church.

Maciel arrived to the Encounter on a beat up Chrysler. It caught my attention because he always traveled in full-size Mercedes Benz vehicles. We were told that it was the best car for his injured back... from his life of penance. And just like that, we learned to focus on his saintly attributes, and never to criticize, not even ponder for a second in our head, what could be narcissism and an abuse of power.

The sad reality is that we get too used to *the privileges* of the clergy. Many of us see and treat priests as superhumans, which leads them to see themselves as superhumans as well... an "imagined identity" that fosters a wrong sense of entitlement. Many of them—like Maciel, but to different degrees—govern their lives by their own set of rules... above the rest of us "regular" humans.

Chapter 14

DEALING WITH THE NEWS

As a school district supervisor, I soon learned that the job calls you to wear many hats. That morning, I substituted a colleague teacher, and taught her Advanced Placement Spanish class, a high school course that offers three college credits. As I entered the classroom early in the morning, and I turned to the white board to make some notes, I realized someone had drawn a man-bird on the board. It was beautiful, muscular, but with a beak and big black extended wings.

"We have an artist in the class– it's beautiful," I said, in Spanish and added: "Would the artist like to identify himself or herself?"

The class was composed of a mixed population: boys and girls, seemingly from different racial backgrounds. A thin boy with black disheveled hair sitting in the back raised his hand.

"Thank you… Mr…?"

"Valencia," he said.

"Mr. Valencia, are you a senior?"

"Yes."

"He is going to Brown in the fall, Ms. Sada… he's going to be an artist," a petite blond girl in the classroom said.

"Congratulations! You *are* an artist. Stay in touch… And let's make sure you all get your three college credits from this class. Ms. Gerald is sick and I will be teaching the class."

The man-black-bird was another stupid coincidence, so I erased it from the board and from my mind and began: "La vida de Lazarillo de Tormes and Joven mendigo." I wrote both titles on the white board where there were no more signs of a bird's silhouette.

"You read a very meaningful excerpt inferencing Lazarillo's main traits. You tried to understand his motivations and values in small groups using a Socratic model. Now we are taking our analysis a step further. With your thinking partner, we will compare the following theme in both works. Your focus will be: the representation of childhood manifested in both the text and the painting." I wrote the focus and continued: "Tools that you will need: First…" I pointed to the board and the students read: the rubric. "Yes," I continued, "It is a rubric you created and you know what a complete comparison would entail by now… please use the rubric to check your work." I pointed at the poster with the rubric. "So let's say that I am starting the comparison. What do you think I will do first?... Don't answer yet. I want you to think, and when you are ready to give an answer, turn your card green-side up. When your partner has done the same, then you can share your answer." I had passed the cards to each student; green on one side and yellow on the other. The yellow meant that the students needed time to think.

After a few minutes, I asked, "Who has a suggestion?"

A student raised his hand and said, "We think that we should first identify the epoch and the genre for each work."

I felt pleased; students need to identify their individual voices.

"Thank you. If you agree, please raise your hand and be ready to explain why.

In the same fashion, I went through the room and collected a few answers until every team had shared.

I wrote: "Picaresque" and added: "From the word picaro…the child in the kitchen in charge of 'picar' or 'to chop' the vegetables for the stew… the cook's helper… who, as he helps, eats the food… because he is hungry, and he is poor. So eating food that was not his was considered misbehavior… and that is where the term 'picaro' got its meaning, and where the genre got its name: picaresque. This will be your reference genre. Think of the epoch, what was happening in Spain and in Europe during that time, and why is it that in our picaresque representations—whether in writing or in a painting—the picaro is a hero? ...And therefore, how do these two heroes differ?" I asked as I circled the titles and drew a couple of arrows in the "thinking map" I had created on the board to model my thinking process and represent what I was saying.

For most of the students in this class, Spanish was the only AP course they could take. They were not—in general—high-achieving students. Also, most of them came from low-income households, so the topic of the 'picaro' was something that genuinely intrigued them.

After 15 minutes of brainstorming and shared writing, the bell rang and the students and I started to get ready to leave. It was Friday afternoon and I stopped by the main office to drop off a note for Ms. Gerald. That is when I saw it: a picture of Maciel and a May 19, 2006, New York Times article: The Vatican Punishes a Leader After Abuse Charges. I grabbed the paper and read. The article concluded by saying that the Legionaries, now based in Connecticut, released a statement noting that Father Maciel has long declared his innocence, and "had decided not to defend himself, following the example of Jesus."

They were still denying it. It would take the order four more years before they could publicly admit that Maciel was a pedophile and a thief.

In an attempt to put the pieces together, many of us—former Legion and RC members— spoke often; some even created support groups. We counted on each other to try to find answers to our questions. I was one of the lucky ones who had health insurance though work and, thus, I had a therapist. My sessions should have begun as soon as I left the movement, but I was still "trained" to doubt modern psychology, so I did not look for counseling until I was already suffering in my marriage.

Between 2006 and 2008, the *new* social media tool, Facebook, became available to anyone who had a valid email address. We "came together" on Facebook to share our reflections and experiences. Other friends—not former RC members—would sometimes join the conversations. I took part in some of them because I wanted to decipher my blackbird symbolism and coincidence: did the others feel like victims, or like traders? Was I—the recruiter—a trader? What happened to us during those years that was so hard to "shake off?"

Rick: What I don't understand is why and how Maciel got away with his crimes... Did you guys know that only 25 years ago, Ratzinger, the current Pope—while he was Prefect of the Congregation of the Faith— excommunicated Cardinal Lefebvre, the French cardinal, just for ordaining three bishops without the Pope's permission? He was freaking excommunicated for ordaining a bishop! How come, Maciel, a pedophile and thief, is just asked to retire and live a life of penance? And so, he goes to live in a beautiful property on the Florida Gulf Coast, with a $20,000 monthly budget? Please, someone explain this to me.

Pat: I think that Msgr. Cicero, the one in charge of the investigation at the Vatican, was not happy about it... Certain sources told me that he had been trying to nail Maciel since 1998 when evidence arrived to Ratzinger's office, but Serrano, the Secretary of State, and Somalo, Prefect of the Congregation for Religious Orders, considered the investigation "ridiculous." Here are my two cents: Lefebvre's disobedience was a public act...Maciel's was still covered up under bills... I mean, under the rug. Also, everyone was trying to protect John Paul II's reputation—the poor man was so very old.

Rick: It is clear Ratzinger messed it up, since Maciel deserved excommunication and jail.

Pat: It's clear that Ratzinger lost sleep over this for years, and as soon as JPII died and he was elected Pope, he saw his chance to open the case, which he did immediately. Give the man some credit.

Rick: Now that the shit is hitting the fan, and the order is still in denial, he probably sees he should have given the evidence to the corresponding authorities so they could prosecute Maciel.

Pat: Maciel just died, what good would that do?

Rick: Maybe the members will open their eyes.

Then Pat had told Rick that he couldn't know because he hadn't been a member. To which Rick said that he could tell Pat had been one. Pat had wrapped up the conversation with a smiley face.

Pat had a point—Rick wouldn't understand the "painful and slow brainwashing reversal process."

I heard a knock on the door. It was my sister, Clara, the one who visited me in New York when I first settled there, and the one who always watched over me like a mother. "Are you working?"

"No," I replied, "just reading notes in Facebook."

William and I were spending spring break in Monterrey, and we were staying at my parents' home.

As she approached the desk, she placed her hand on my shoulder. Only my siblings and a few close friends knew the turmoil in which I still lived. Maciel's recent death, instead of bringing healing, had opened wounds—people were divided, many were angry and frustrated, others were in denial.

Clara left reminding me that we would meet for dinner.

I browsed another post.

Juan: Elena, how can you excuse Legion priests like your cousin, Javier? He had to know about Maciel's crimes, and he treated some people like shit.

Elena: I don't excuse Javier... I don't excuse myself either. Just keep in mind that Maciel trained the priests in the order. I agree that we are still responsible for our acts; what I am saying is that, at least I cannot judge anymore unless I am a first witness... because what I thought was a lie (Maciel's crimes) turned out to be true, and what I defended as truth (his sanctity and the madness of his accusers) turned out to be a lie.

Juan: OK, so let's just look at the facts. Javier knew about the mistress, Sarah, and the daughter she and Maciel had. It is public knowledge... They were seen together...along with some of your former colleagues.

Elena: He suspected it like some of us later did. Javier found out through an investigation he conducted on his own initiative... Don't forget that he had to follow orders too—*Oboedientia Perfecta*...

James: Maciel used to brag... though at the time we didn't think of it as "bragging"... about being able to get fake passports for priests who were persecuted in the Soviet bloc. I guess he got a couple of his own since, if I am not mistaken, that is how Javier found out about the daughter: he discovered Maciel's passport with his Pseudo name—Marcial Rivero. They were in Florida... Maciel had already been "suspended" from the order, and his mind was pretty "gone" by then.

Elena: I believe that is what triggered the investigation, which according to Javier was after the Vatican "suspended" Maciel. Rivero was also the last name of their daughter, whom he had introduced as the daughter of a Spanish benefactor. Javier and others started to put the pieces of the puzzle together... But even then, they couldn't talk much about it. Remember the private promise? And it was "just" about having a daughter; had he not committed the other crimes, it would not have been devastating... having a child out of wedlock, as "wrong" as it might be for Catholic priests, it is not a crime.

Lucy: Maciel—the jerk—would use donations to eat and sleep with his harem in five-star hotels, while we saved every penny, because it was money given to the poor!

"How well did you get to know Maciel?" One of my sisters-in-law, asked as soon as my parents left the table to go to rest in their bedroom. It was our typical Sunday night dinner. My sisters and I have had the chance to talk about Maciel, but I hadn't spoken about it with the rest of the siblings and in-laws.

I struggled but said: "He was a perverse abusive narcissist who created his own reality."

"What do you mean?" she asked.

"Well, it's a pathology. Abusive narcissists choose victims who, in their eyes, are aggressors... and he sucks the life out of them. Then, they use that source of energy to appear like a powerful and perfect leader before everyone else. Hitler was the extreme case."

To which Carlotta, a sister, added: "Well, you know that abusive narcissists become that because they are smart and when they are young... and it's time to 'come out' of the natural narcissist childlike personality... they instead create a reality to avoid an unbearable pain."

"So it's a coping mechanism?" a brother asked.

"Exactly," Carlotta replied, and added. "They have no conscience or remorse... and they are in denial all their life. That's why it is so hard to help them in therapy... Also, they justify their wrongdoing by creating their own rules. They think they are entitled."

I had missed those family dinners for 17 years. "How many dinners does that add up to?" one of the brothers had asked when talking about how nice it was to have me home. "Close to 1,000," five family members replied immediately and at the same time.

The interrogation continued but at least it happened as I predicted... Even if I wanted to answer all their questions, I couldn't sneak a word in edgewise. Nothing had really changed—many talked and a few listened. The thought gave me a sense of security: I am familiar with everything at home... even the interruption patterns. *Nice... I will not have to reply.* It is the overwhelming beauty of family love that I was lucky to experience... Not perfect love, but still family love. The thought made me smile again. And I kept eating... while everyone talked.

Chapter 15

The Hullabaloo

That same year, in July, I visited Monterrey again. It was joyful, but still difficult. Maciel's crimes were well known by now and friends and relatives assumed I left RC because I knew about his double life. I was constantly drilled with questions. It had been indescribably tough news for my mother. She had loved Maciel and had trusted him, as most RC members had. She had been one of the first ones in town to welcome the Legionary priest into her home. The "poor man"—a Legionary priest—had the misfortune of getting a flat tire outside of our gate. "Divine coincidence," the priest had explained. Mom had been instrumental in the establishment of their first community in the city. She had even convinced my father, and some of his relatives, to sponsor their new schools in Monterrey. She admired Maciel's priestly dedication and the way his "works" were helping her be a better mother and wife. She was definitely more patient, caring, and devoted after she was introduced to RC. On the other hand, Dad had followed a different path. Raised, for part of his life in New England, he was more skeptical... He had not agreed with Maciel on several occasions. He had even shared his disapproval, which scandalized me in the past. I had taken a vow to never criticize a superior... my father hadn't. I had to remind myself of that. The bottom line was: my father did not consider it ethical to conceal the Legion's schools' financial reports. Even if they were private schools, they—nevertheless—were not for profit. Besides, one of the schools was still in his name. So when the Vatican admonished Maciel, and shit hit the fan, Dad was terribly sad, but not as shocked as the rest of us in the family had been. We grew up thinking the man was a saint. He didn't.

One day during lunch, my mother asked how I was doing. "You know, with everything that is now in the open about Father Maciel…"

"Shocked, but alright," I said. "You?" She shook her head and said no more.

My dad gave me a sympathetic smile and asked, "How is New York?" It didn't surprise me that he wanted to spare my mom the pain.

The roles had reversed; my mom was now the one keeping silence. During my first years in RC, while living in Rome, my parents came to see me. Had I told Dad how I felt, he would have taken me home immediately. I did tell Mom, but she had already been "affected" by the *RC mentality,* so her advice was: "You have a vocation unless the directors tell you otherwise." She also suggested not telling Dad about my doubts, since he could worry. So I kept my feelings to myself. Now, she was the one keeping her feelings to herself and my heart wept for her.

Years later, Mom and I spoke about this and forgave each other. I forgave her for having been so involved in RC that she lost sight of the degree to which we both had renounced our own judgment. I apologized to her for having judged her harshly. The reality is that she could only see the happy facade I presented the few times we met during those 18 years; and, since my letters were read—and many times, retained—by directors before being mailed, she never saw the depth of my anguish.

Dad's analytical personality, together with the fact that he had distanced himself from RC –not on purpose, but because he was a busy business, civic, and philanthropic man—had served him well. Also, his reserved and "composed" personality was so notorious that friends would joke that probably a British family had left him in a basket at his parents' doorsteps... or even... that his mother, Mrs. Beatriz Sada, must have had an affair with a British aristocrat... which, of course, was ridiculous and impossible. Not only was Dad a carbon copy of his father, Grandfather—or Pane—Andres, but she was her husband's "guardian angel"... always by his side. Sophisticated and cheerful Grandma Beatriz—whom we called Mane Chata—had been the fortunate recipient of the best her Mexican, French, Andalusian, and Jewish ancestors could offer. Her dark eyes and smile would turn heads. She was beautiful inside and out, and she didn't seem to know it. Her husband—Pane Andres, a blue-eyed, impeccably dressed, caring, and successful husband— had nothing to worry about. Mane Chata loved him dearly. She also loved the "hullabaloo" of all 29 of us grandchildren, with the girls' drama and the boys' destructive powers; she loved and appreciated the unshakable calmness of one daughter as much as the excitement of the other; the militant spirit of a daughter-in-law as much as the flexibility of the other... a son's bohemian soul as much as my dad's reserved and "composed" personality.

Pane and Mane lived in the same compound with all of us... that is, with their six children –each in their own home—and their children's children. When there was an "incident" caused by one of us in someone else's home, she used to say: "Today, a nephew or niece destroyed your garden, tomorrow it will be one of yours... so it is all the same." Though no one really knew where one property started and the other ended... no one even knew which dog or cat belonged to whom; pets kept getting fat after collecting food from everyone's kitchen.

My family was not even dysfunctional... It was actually "normal." Pane Andres was one of 16, and Mane, one of eight... So it had been as "normal" as it can be with more than 100 second cousins living in town... most within five miles. It had been "normal" for me, since it was the only type of childhood I knew until I turned 10. With so many cousins around, a pool and a private playground... playdates with school kids were not as appealing. The only friend's house I visited before I started fifth grade was my classmate's, Teresa. She had two horses in her backyard and I loved riding them. We did not have horses at home, only at the Buenos Aires Ranch, outside of Linares, Tamaulipas. It was a working ranch where we had learned to ride horses, milk goats, bathe

the pigs, and where we had to be reminded not to swim in the cattle's water supply tank, or swing from the orange trees.

The property where we lived had been officially named by Mane: "The Hullabaloo." So our postal mail sometimes mistakenly read: The Hullabaloo, our street's name, Monterrey... and somehow letters would reach their destination. By the pool, there was a patio and a charming sitting area where adults would sit with an evening tequila or highball whiskey.

It was there where we—kids—who were supposed to be oblivious to adult conversations, had learned most family secrets and interesting facts. It was there where... while collecting miniature frogs and creating mud islands—an alleged ants' resort... that I learned where and why my parents traveled so often while we were young. They traveled—mainly—to help the business generate more jobs, and to participate in innumerable social promotion events. My parents had an extraordinary awareness of their civic duties, and they always did what was in Mexico's best interest. Growing up, I reflected often on the loneliness I felt during their trips. Their leadership roles and duty had cost me many days of a certain heart emptiness, running to my parents' bedroom after school, only to remember they wouldn't be back for days. But, now, as an adult, I have come to understand it and accept it—since, somehow, it didn't take away from the love they gave each of us.

My Mom and Dad were true partners in many ways. I remember a day Dad got a standing ovation after a speech; he had to speak in public often since he had been chosen to represent the Mexican private industry during a time when the government was taking over industries, when Presidents Luis Echeverria and Lopez Portillo almost destroyed the country's economy. As everyone got up and applauded, I looked at my mother. I could only see her profile from a lower angle, since I was just a girl... but I could tell she was radiant and her eyes were teary. Maybe I was the only one in that huge auditorium that knew she had helped Dad rewrite parts of the speech. I sometimes tried to picture her as the CEO of a large company, and I actually could picture her perfectly, together with two or three of my aunts. I always wondered if women of their generation experienced a longing for a professional career. How fast everything had changed from one generation to the next, and how open minded they had to be to accept the changes in their children's lives since it affected their sons as much as their daughters. With no doubt, public access to mass media had a huge role in this schema shift... when my mom was born, the TV had not yet been invented.

Monterrey's weather would allow, almost year round, those gatherings in the pool-side patio that Pane Andres had the vision to build.

I miss Pane Andres and Mane Chata terribly every time I visit Monterrey. I never met my mom's father, and I loved her mom very much as well. Nevertheless, I got to see Andres and Chata the most. They passed away during the years that followed my departure for Rome when I joined RC, and I never got closure to my longing for them... I never mourned their deaths. RC, or the priest in charge of us in Rome, had not given me permission to travel to their funerals. "You might be tempted and your vocation might suffer," he explained. I did not even fight it... I just ran to the orchard after making up the excuse that I had left the water running and I needed to go back to shut it off. There, under a fig tree, where no one could see me or hear me, I let my tears run free.

And as I soaked my feet in The Hullabaloo pool, only two days after my arrival to Monterrey for a visit during the scorching month of July, I could reconstruct the scenes with Pane and Mane, aunts, uncles and cousins... and hear them all, except my dear Mane and Pane. With sadness, I remembered what I read once: when someone dies, their voice is the first thing we forget. I said a prayer and thanked them for The Hullabaloo, for the pool, for giving birth to my father, for loving my mother as their own daughter... and for granting me such a magnificent legacy of tender and affectionate love and joy.

Hearing that Maciel spent time with his two illegitimate families while we were deprived of it made many of us feel angry. The anger intensified when we thought about how we could not bring back those that we had not been allowed to bury.

~ ~ ~ ~

I am wearing one of the six outfits I am allowed to use in RC: a long skirt, a button-down blouse, and black shoes. I stand, looking at the dead body of an old woman. An elongated white marvel statue of a young woman holding a dove looks down on the lifeless body... It is a memorial by a tombstone. I recognize the cadaver. It is Maura, Maciel's mother—Mamá Maurita. I cry as I remember the sweet old lady... now pale... almost gray. There is sadness in her expression... Did Maura realize with that mysterious awareness of the dead that her son had not made it to her burial? "Don't be sad," I tell her. "I am sure your son is running some important errand for God... Otherwise, he would be here," I add, hoping her soul can still hear me. Maura's eyes open... two concave circles in her sockets... and she moans. I jump back, terrified. The woman lets out a loud and strenuous groan from a motionless opened mouth. It comes like piercing thunder... a groan that never stops... it just fades away.

I woke up shaking... A thunderstorm had actually disrupted my sleep.

Mama Maurita died without saying goodbye to her son. She had even been buried without Maciel. And it had nothing to do with the rules Maciel himself had imposed...which prevented members from burying their loved ones. It was just that... he was nowhere to be found. No one knew his whereabouts. How could a man adored and followed by thousands get so... lost. "I was taking care of a delicate matter, something the Holy Father had asked me to do in absolute confidentiality," he had explained on the phone when he called to make arrangements for his transportation from the airport, before his secretary could inform him that Maura had been dead and buried for almost a week. "Oh... that is the type of person our Father Founder is," my superior had explained, once the news of his heroic action started to travel around the world. "Just like the Gospel says: 'Let the dead bury the dead, and come and follow me...' He always places the needs of the Church first... above all personal needs... above what his heart would want. We should follow the example of this saintly man God placed as our guide and model."

It later became known that Maciel had been sipping the best wines and staying at a five-star hotel on the coast of France when Maura died and during the days that followed... True, he was out of reach for everyone... except for the woman on his bed. *Twisted hypocrite...* No human person can be an absolute model... no matter how much he or she is worshiped.

Chapter 16

A Cult

It is often said that during the fall, trees lose their leaves since the imminent harsh winter, either the coldness or dryness, destroys them. However, that is not exactly true. It is not the weather—an outside factor—but, rather, the trees themselves that shed their leaves as a survival strategy. Trees live the life they intend to live, by letting go of their leaves. They lose their leaves in the winter as a survival strategy; it does not pay off to keep them—the energy spent keeping them alive is greater than the energy produced by the leaves during the cold months. Also, since the sun is not as intense, the plants' roots do not need the shade. During this time, trees—except for evergreens—store their energy through 'abscission,' which literally means 'to cut,' and from which English adopts the term 'scissors'...I acquired 16 credits in linguistics at Hunter College, which—in combination with my philosophy and language courses from my 'previous life'—produced the 'word junkie' that I am today.

By the winter of 2010, I was working for New Rochelle's school district, in New York, as an ESL and Dual Language Programs Supervisor. We had moved from our 650 square-feet Manhattan apartment, to an apartment slightly bigger in Bronxville, NY, a charming Manhattan commuters' suburb 10 minutes from my office. Joseph was already two; and we were getting ready to—potentially—adopt Sandra, who was three and still in the orphanage because some of Mexico's adoption practices are archaic.

As I contemplated the change in the trees' foliage outside my office, I reflected on the "abscission" my soul produced in my life that winter, which had helped me survive. I had finally cut Maciel's erroneous teachings, which led to the realization that even though Regnum Christi and the Legion were a legitimate teaching and apostolic Catholic group, they had also been—potentially, still were—cults.

Cults come in different shapes and sizes, as author Dr. Janja Lalich states in her book *Take Back Your Life*—a book I stumbled upon as I was finishing writing this one and which I highly recommend. The stories I heard about modern-day cults captivate me. I find my experience in RC very similar to that of "victims" in other groups. There are many, like some branches of the Fundamentalist Church of Jesus Christ of Latter Day (FLDS), and of Jehovah Witnesses, World Peace and Unification Sanctuary, The Twelve Tribes, NXIVM, United Nation of Islam, Children of God, etc. Many of these have been featured in several documentaries, including a documentary series aired in A&E, where Dr. Lalich gives her expert opinion. Some are religion based; others—like NXIVM and Charles Manson's community—follow a godlike leader. Most of these groups have hundreds or thousands of followers. Others, as was the case with Elizabeth Smart's kidnapper, only have a handful or fewer followers. In some cases, victims are born into the group; and in others, members join, mostly deceived by an astute, abusive narcissist (or a group of them), who takes advantage of the person's altruistic or spiritual desires. NXIVM, for example, presents itself as a self-help group that recruits and prepares some of the best leaders in the world. It recruited very smart and altruistic individuals, including a former Mexican President's son, Emiliano Salinas—who resigned his membership two weeks after the founder, Keith Raniere, was arrested on sex-trafficking charges.

Cults isolate the members and "empty" them of their beliefs to "fill" them with new ones; beliefs that lead them to set aside their judgment and submit to the group leader. The process does not seem radical at the beginning; it is carefully crafted to happen in increasing doses. If the group commits a covered-up crime (though it might not feel like a crime), you, the member, are positioned to be the perpetrator or, at least, the accomplice. Then you are committed—you become one of them—and you don't see your way out. The reason why immoral or illicit actions don't seem to be "bad" actions is because by the time you witness them, you believe and trust in the leaders, but not in yourself. Even those who arrived to RC after living accomplished lives in Wall Street, academia, or other secular and intellectually challenging sectors, would—by their second year of "formation"—ask how to chop carrots because their old ways are not the right ways. You get to believe that the group's rules and practices have been tested and lead to fulfillment, a worthy venue for your altruistic dreams.

I was an assertive girl growing up. One day during dinner, Pane Andres announced it to the rest of the family. He explained that he had seen me under a tree by the ranch's creek. I was only eight and I was in a squat showing Colorado, my favorite horse, a group of squiggly tadpoles swimming carefree in the water. I was talking and Colorado was listening. I asked him if he had eaten a tadpole by accident…because it was hard to avoid them due to their squiggly motions in the water right under the animal's nose. Pane told everyone during the family dinner that night, that with a nod and a snort, the horse had responded affirmatively to my question. Pane had also said that I carried on the conversation with the animal, assuring him that the tadpoles would not turn into frogs inside of him, and that they were a good source of protein… and protein was important for the muscles… "Besides, there are already too many frogs in the ranch," I had taken the time to explain to the horse. Everyone at the table had laughed, especially Uncle Gerardo… my funny uncle. I remembered I had joined in their laughter because I also thought a dinner plate with tadpoles would be funny. "She is an assertive girl," Pane had added. Indeed, I had been a very assertive little girl. I had lost it with age. Many things had happened… Many years of needing to justify myself "had happened."

I joined Regnum Christi because I wanted to make life better for children who did not "have my good fortune." I wanted to open schools, teach, and preach. Maciel tapped into my ambition and recruited me in my teens. I had heard the Pope say he loved Maciel (first in Rome, and then in the Philippines). He—supposedly—had approved all of our rules and practices and had praised them as an effective way to reach holiness and serve humanity.

One of the cult-detox cases I heard was that of Caroline Jessop. I was especially captivated by it, maybe because Caroline fled a Fundamentalist Later-Day Saints (FLDS) group based in Texas shortly after I left RC. I read her books and heard her speak years later. As I read her books, I woke up to the realization that RC was a cult. Even though our circumstances were different—she was in a polygamous relationship, and I lived in abstinence—we both experienced deprivation of our judgment and our rights, the feeling of being trapped, and the pain of knowing we had brought loved ones into an abusive system. I knew she could understand me, which didn't happen often when I spoke about being in RC.

Caroline had the courage to flee from one of the most extreme FLDS communities in the country, in which her husband was the leader. Caroline's emotionally abusive and polygamist husband had been charged in a court and sentenced to life in prison. I still wondered why Maciel had not been charged in the same way, and was buried, after his death in 2008, by hundreds of fans and followers.

Chapter 17

Everyone Deserves a Second Chance

No one joins a cult. I did not join a cult. I joined RC because I did not know it was a cult. Maciel deceived us. In 2010, most of us admitted that—without denying the good works of the group—RC was a cult, or at least, had all the cult elements: leadership that commits crimes, is adored, cannot be criticized, and has no accountability; a caste system where the leader is at the very top of the pyramid and is untouchable; a structure with informants or spies, and that forbids communication between subjects, and between these and their families; a culture where the leader undermines other systems, including one's own family, and uses guilt for control; and protocols that ration sleep, nourishment, and rest.

"I am not sure if I can be of any help, Laura! It has been only a year since the 'curtain fell' for me," I said. It had taken me 10 years to completely 'deprogram' myself—mind and heart—from Maciel's ways.

Laura, like many other RC members I love dearly, was still in RC, and had called me on the phone to ask for help.

"What are you talking about? You are ahead of the game; most of us are still in RC, and… it's hard to think straight!" she exclaimed before pleading once again: "Please Elena, just meet with him. He will be in the States in a few weeks."

I did not want to do it. What was the point of meeting with Archbishop Blazquez, the papal appointee to assess the RC communities around the world? If he was anything like Cardinal de Paolis—the Vatican official assigned to run the Legion and RC while they cleaned up the mess—it would be a waste of time. De Paolis never recognized the deep cleansing the Legion and RC needed.

When I did not reply, Laura added: "He has been in most of our centers, listening to people and asking questions."

"How do we know that he's not one more bureaucrat who will use the visits to boost his ego and take what we say as hysteria? Let's face it—who doesn't want to be received as king in a house inhabited by dozens of beautiful woman who cook and sing for you?" My stomach flipped just remembering the "show" we had to prepare every time some important clerical figure would visit our centers. If the Church's hierarchy feel and act like superhumans, it is our fault; we encourage those feelings and behaviors that, ultimately, lead them to feel entitled to create the rules by which they live, instead of submitting to the rules all humans follow.

"We don't know yet, but it is the only thing we can do at this point. Elena, please."

"What for?" I continued. "Based on many of my conversation with some of you, seemingly—in general, and as a community—the female branch wants to remain under the Legionary priests' jurisdiction. And… it is their lives, their norms… they should be the ones redefining them, and no one else. I'm not part of it anymore… thank God." I regretted that last statement. I needed to be more empathetic.

"But how on earth can we do that effectively if we are still programed under the abusive belief system and—seemingly—we don't even know it?"

"So what do you expect… that they will believe someone from outside who comes in and says: 'Just trust me'? Laura, we were taught that it was God's will for us to show claws if someone criticizes our life… since it was inspired by the Holy Spirit! You know that…"

"Elena, you have two cousins in the Legion. They have important roles; your family still has ties with RC. You were vocational director for 10 years in North America. He will listen to you."

Deep down, I knew Laura was right; there were still good people in RC and they deserved the right to give it a good fight. Only if they were truly open to change would they survive. My beloved friend and former colleague waited.

"I'll tell you something," I finally said. "I will write to him. If after that, he wants to meet, I will meet... though I doubt it. Have you forgotten I was exiled to the Wild West for the sake of damage control?" I said, referring to my exile to California.

We laughed... we could now laugh about those years together.

I wrote to Archbishop Blazquez: *"As I watched on T.V. a special report on John Paul II's future and expected beatification, I remembered the day when, during a private audience, the deceased Pontiff told me, 'I love your Father Founder, Father Maciel, very much'. That day, the benefactor I was accompanying during the audience donated to Maciel one million dollars 'for a cause in his heart.' As I reflect on what we know now about Father Maciel's life, I grieve thinking about the number of people who felt deceived and betrayed by him.*

I am not sure if what I will write in this letter will even be considered. I do it thinking I owe it to those who were deceived and who, without knowing it, are still suffering the consequences of his abuses and lies..."

In my letter, I told the archbishop about myself, about my roles, and my experiences. I told him how the women in RC should be able to vote and choose their own leadership. I tried to articulate as best I could how the "short-leash" culture was one the founder established to serve his own selfish purposes, but that it killed us emotionally. I told him I had serious concerns about the competitive spirit fostered within the movement thanks to the way the founder—and now superiors—praise the members' capacity to recruit and raise money as if there was a correlation between their "accomplishments" and their sanctity... which is mere manipulation. I also told him about my experience in the field of financial accountability. Though individual members had to be accountable in detail, schools and other RC institutions hid financial reports following the founder's orders... never allowing deserved salary increases to lay people involved. This spirit prevailed after Maciel was removed as director. Finally, I told him how it had taken me almost 10 years to understand the extent of the founder's influence on the movement, and that it would be extremely hard for someone to see this from within.

Archbishop Blazquez's secretary received my letter and thanked me for it. Months later, the document he turned in at the Vatican with his recommendations reflected my suggestions and many more; nevertheless, they were practically dismissed by Cardinal Velasio de Paolis. There was a vote indeed, but with the excuse that it was simply a "recommendation." The ballots completed by the women choosing their leaders were read... but mostly shelved by the superior-priests in the Legion. Ultimately, those women who remained preferred to be under the priests' authority... since choosing independence would be prideful and would show a lack of unity. It was the only way they knew how to live... who could blame them? It reminded me of stories where spouses stay in marriages even when the other spouse is abusive... because it is the only "way" they know how to live... because they think their relationship is "the norm." They bear it until something or someone outside opens their eyes. And even then, it is hard to accept and to escape.

I read Laura's email sent from a Gmail account. She told me about the voting process. She asked me to be prudent, since she knew about it only because someone else—who had been entrusted as secretary—had confided in her. I felt empathy for those whose eyes had been open... since the ones who were still blind were probably oblivious to the pain they "ought" to suffer.

During my first year out of RC, my main learning experience was that I could not change the world; instead, I could be happy and help others be happy by simply being myself... and by loving them. I could not soothe—not even with my notes and prayer—the bitterness of some ex-members, the blackbirding victims.

I tried to apply what I learned in the process to my current relationships, including those at work. I began to notice how, everywhere around me, people impose their judgment as "the best judgment." Even teachers did it with the way they taught history, civics, and language. My area of expertise—language—was a pretty "safe" area, since it supposedly abstains from ideologies and agenda. I was wrong. Even language teachers impose our judgment when we transmit the message that Standard English is the "correct" language... when it is just that: the standard language.

When I was working for the New York City Department of Education's Chancellor, my boss was a woman with a Harvard PhD in Education. She told me I could not work for her if I was not voting Democrat—I was, and still am, registered as an Independent voter. Later, while working as a supervisor in a school district, during the 2009 economic crisis, when I expressed my preference to freeze our raises in order to prevent lay-offs, my union leader asked me to "keep my pretty mouth shut."

People all around us impose their judgment.

In 2013, a priest who had been a supervisor in the Legion wrote a letter that I think encompassed what most of us wanted to say as we wrapped our heads around RC chapters—of abuse and healing—in our lives.

Someone in the Legion made Father Deomar's letter public. It was someone who had access to the Legion's archives and decided it deserved to be made public. It was addressed to the order's General Director, Father Corcuera. Maciel appointed Corcuera (in a supposed voting process), when he resigned after Pope John Paul II's death.

Maciel anticipated that after the Pope's death, Ratzinger would "sentence" him to retire to a life of prayer and penance, and he prepared us by stepping down as General Director, and telling us that "something terrible" would happen to test his sanctity and the endurance and faith of the members.

Deomar had been a successful Brazilian engineer for several years before he became a priest in the Legion. He had done his philosophical and theological studies in Rome and, since then, had been assigned as a superior of several Legionary seminaries in Spain, Argentina, Mexico, and Brazil. The letter became popular fast, because he was widely respected and very well known. He had been one of Maciel's loyal leaders. His advantage over most of the other priests was that he joined the Legion older—early 30s instead of teens. He was an exception, and his work led him to interact constantly with the Church hierarchy, who had "wider" viewpoints.

Father Deomar started the letter by stating that he was offering some reflections. Indeed, reflection, which literally means to give back light or an image, or—in its abstract use—give back an idea or thought in response to a comment or an episode in life, is what the order needed. Maciel's deceit was a monumental episode in our life.

He wrote:

> "When we found out that the accusations against our founder were true, along with the system of concealment created to protect him, I began to question "our belief system," of which I had become part, and with which I collaborated. I had been told we ought to live in total obedience, so I never considered questioning it. Then I began to see how this same "belief system" had manipulated my judgment. And like most superiors in the Legion, I had to psych myself up to believe that the institution was worth more than the person: if you contradict or even question the "belief system," you are

discarded. And so… men and women who had been members for 30 years were dismissed almost as evil people and were asked by their superiors to leave the congregation.

That happened to me, too. When I started to present my ideas and my way of thinking, I was isolated… I couldn't preach retreats or teach workshops anymore. I can even see how the concept of "total obedience" was exercised wrongly… Religious life in the Church requires freedom and not manipulation.

My frustration increased as I saw that those making the decisions in the Legion were precisely the ones who were part of the "belief system" we inherited from the founder, and that there was little acceptance of the immensity of the 'cleanup' that needed to take place in order to survive."

Deomar concluded his letter with a plea for change.

The letter summarized my own reflections perfectly… and based on everyone's comments on my post, as I disseminated the English translation of the letter, it summarized the reflections of many people.

By providing our feedback, I believe that we gave the order a second chance, in the same way destiny had given me, Deomar, and many others, a second chance.

Part III

Living the Life That I Intend to Live

Chapter 18

PATRIMONY

My plane took off and flew between the rocky mountains of northern Mexico and the Sierra Madre, ranges that create the valley where Monterrey was built. My mind traveled to the beautiful Blue Ridge Mountains in North Carolina. I had come across them through a casual Google search, and when I read about them, about their thousands of bike and hiking trails, of their horses and vineyards, they called to me. Since the, I visited them and they felt like home. Maybe one day they will be my home. They are 1500 miles northeast from my dear Monterrey mountains, yet they seem to have a similar DNA. The 5,700-foot-high Cerro de la Silla (or Saddle Hill) extends to the east of Monterrey, only 900 feet short of reaching the Blue Ridge's highest peak, Mount Mitchell, the highest peak in the eastern United States.

The beautiful Monterrey mountain range disappeared, and I said: "See you on the other side." Then the vast Texan flatness took over past the Rio Grande: a manmade line that made Sierra Madre and me from one country, and Blue Ridge and my children from another. My ancestors had been in the same situation. They also adopted other nationalities and cultures. Why was this hard? Patriotism had always been a very important value in my family among both sides of my family. My ancestors had fought for Mexico's independence where a Texan and American flag was now swaying. A 21-year-old Spaniard, Manuel Sada, had arrived to New Spain in the 18th century, as a loyal emissary of the King of Spain. And when he fell in love and married the great-grand daughter of Captain Juan Cavazos del Campo, ancestor of one of the leading families in the construction of Mexico's military independence, a family with at least one dozen captains and sergeants, as well as a Governor, Manuel knew there would be no boat back to Spain. In fact, two of their sons joined the army and were generals, and when Mexico plotted its independence from Spain, both accepted to lead armies against their father's army... against men from their father's land: Navarra. So Manuel made the new land his new home. It was his home and his wife's home, the home of his children and his descendants. "Defend what belongs to you and belong to what you defend," he told his two sons, generals. But Manuel Sada did not fight that war... He couldn't conceive fighting with Spain against his own blood... flesh of his flesh. Instead, he blessed his sons' decision to fight. Sons in the army of a new country, fighting against their father's army—not an unusual situation during an independence war. Manuel decided that if Spain considered him a traitor, it was Spain's problem, not his. However, since Mexico won, he remained an expatriate in the land that became his home.

You were so courageous! Wherever you all are... thank you! I told my ancestors. I looked up at the clouds. How wonderful it is to follow the voice in one's heart... Manuel and his descendants did. "When a conscience is not 'well formed,' it is better not to listen to it... It needs a superior to tell the difference between what God wants and what the human lower self is demanding. In your case, Elena, you are suffering from a deformed conscience, so you can't trust the voice in your conscience. God's representative is here to tell you how to act." That had been the verdict given to me during my first year in RC. Somehow, it didn't matter what I did... my conscience never got in shape. *Damn Maciel... What a way to strip youth from their capacity to judge...* And this was typically done once the child had been isolated from their loved ones... *Perverse Maciel.* After that, for 18 years, I could not count on my conscience...I had to ask my superiors about everything. "Who makes a mistake obeying... does not make a mistake at all" Maciel had taught us, and unfortunately, I carried that belief into my marriage.

I was starting to recover my trust in myself... in my capacity to make my own decisions. Manuel and his two sons—one of them, Mathias, Pane Andres' great-grandfather—were not the only examples among my ancestors. There was Francisco, Mathias' son, who resigned his role as a Mexican congressman when the 1845 Mexican Constitution was adopted, forbidding freedom of religion, among other freedoms. There was my great-grand uncle Pablo Sada, who resigned the presidency of Pacific Railroads when Mexican revolutionaries, the cartels of the early 1900s, had demanded the use of the trains to transport stolen "goods," including slaves, children, and women they would rape daily. Finally, there were my parents, who had fought courageously for decades against the expansion of a corrupt government... especially in the 1970s during Echeverria's leadership. During that time, we endured numerous threats against my dad, whose only crime had been to speak the truth publicly.

As the plane continued its trajectory over the clouds, I embraced the new chapter in my life with courage. I couldn't... wouldn't be led by "expectations." I needed to choose my own path. Joseph, my amazing toddler, who had already undergone 12 surgeries since his birth, became my inspiration, leader, and teacher. He taught me to love and to fight for life's joys. Just like my baby had, I needed to accept being vulnerable and to hold onto life's important essential: forgiveness and love of self.

~ ~ ~ ~

Pane Andres places a beautiful turquoise stone surrounded by small diamonds on my hand. "Good luck surrounded by strength. The union of these two stones is very meaningful." His gray and blue eyes stared intently into mine. He looks young... the way he looks in his wedding pictures. He is handsome. "My sweet girl, when you see these two stones, think of the legacy my ancestors and I give you. The turquoise is semi-precious and the diamonds are precious... It is the most enduring stone... But the turquoise will bring good luck... since it will be the type of 'luck' that you build yourself... no one dictates your destiny. You build it. Elena... I love you so very much, sweet girl!" And he was gone... disappeared up in smoke. "No!"

The burning pain in my heart and the yearning for his goodbye hug woke me up. I was on the Monterrey-New York flight. The dream had been so real... Pane Andres did not believe in superstition... and he always believed on building one's own destiny.

The day Pane hugged me goodbye, he hugged the youngest girl of his oldest son. We both knew we would not see each other again in this world. He was suffering of emphysema. Pane and I stood inside the Acapulco airport's terminal, where he and Mane would spend their winters. The humidity seemed to soothe a bit the suffering caused by the emphysema. I had flown from Monterrey to Acapulco that week to spend some days with them before departing for Rome "for good," for seven years, at least. Their health was fragile and no one expected them to travel to Europe to see me. That day, before the horrible "until-heaven-goodbye," he had asked me to go shopping with him at the Princess Hotel. And when we arrived, he handed me money and asked me to buy something, anything I wanted that I could keep and think of him every time I saw it. *Something I could keep...* I had noticed that the RC women had a medal or cross around their neck, which—I was told—they could keep. So I went around the hotel stores looking for a religious medal I could wear around my neck... and that is when I found it. Both Pane and loved it. It was a turquoise medal... a semi-precious stone from the mountains... Perfect! It had an image of a Madonna in the middle. It was a religious medal and, therefore, I could wear it. I put it on... and after that horrific goodbye, I held it tight in my hand. "Bye, Pane. I love you." *I will see you in heaven.* I shed some tears looking through the plane's window. Actually, until the present moment, every time I think about the possibility of dying, I am comforted by the thought that probably I will see my grandparents again… all four of them.

But so it happened that a few weeks after my arrival to Rome, my superior asked me to turn in my turquoise medal.

"When you joined," the woman explained, "you agreed to have 'nothing.' Not even a medal."

I told her the medal had a special meaning.

"More so... you should detach yourself from it," she said. And, resigned, I handed it to her.

Pane's turquoise medal was gone, like everything else in my life. The superior gave me, in exchange, another one... a gold one. A bit bigger, just as pretty... But it had not been in my grandfather's hand... Seemingly, it was an exchange that would foster detachment. I had cried all that day and the following day, thinking about how Pane would feel if he found out. He would be protective of me, no doubt. Maybe he would have taken a plane to Rome and rescued me... But Pane would never find out... at least, not in this life. Some days later, my superior called me to her office and gave me the news. Pane Andres was dead. I asked to attend his funeral, but my request was not granted. I still yearn for my grandparents' embrace.

I arrived home anxious to see the children. I had been in Mexico for almost a week in Mexico. William and I had just celebrated our 10th wedding anniversary and the relationship had taken a turn for the worse.

Chapter 19

TEACHER

During my 10 years of marriage, my greatest joy was my kids. My second joy was my job, especially teaching. I never struggled to understand my identity as a mother. However, I struggled to find my identity in marriage, and even more so at work.

One day, for example, I met some fellow teachers after work to celebrate a birthday. While sitting around a large table, one of the teachers commented on the beer he was drinking—a DOS XX Amber. It was his favorite beer.

"Mine too!" I said, and added nonchalantly: "Did you know that its home brewery, the Cuauhtémoc and later, FEMSA, was the first one in the world to use caps instead of cork on its beers?"

"Wow, how do you know such an interesting fact?" someone asked.

"The... they are based in Monterrey, where I am from," I replied. I did not share that my great-grandfather, Francisco, had come up with the idea after learning about the way Coke was being bottled.

I preferred it that way... they only knew me as a Mexican-American teacher. It wasn't until I started my research on the relationship between identity, language, and academic/professional performance, that I realized how shortsighted I had been. While I was a teacher in New York City, I was granted the opportunity—and scholarship—to pursue a master's degree and an advanced certificate on Supervision and Administration of Schools and School Districts at Hunter College, CUNY. It was then, and later, while acquiring my doctorate on Bilingual and Multicultural Education at the University of Connecticut, that I understood the role that identity has in a person's ability to develop their "imagined identity" and, thus, the "imagined community" they see themselves as part of.

There was—in New York—a student who inspired me to further my academic preparation in the area of bilingual and multicultural education. His name was Pedro, and he was a Mexican-American immigrant from Michoacán, Mexico. Pedro was living with his family in New Rochelle, New York, where the school district had recently welcomed a wave of immigrants from Michoacán, many escaping drug cartel threats on them or their children. This particular population of immigrants is every teacher's dream—they are hard working and extremely motivated to succeed.

One day, Pedro was offering the class a summary of one of the books. He was asked to write the title on the board, but standing by the blackboard in front of the class with chalk on his hand, he froze. He had written *The,* but would not continue with the second word, *Ecosystems.* "Do you need help remembering the title, Pedro? It is OK if you do," I said. "Ecosystems," he replied, but he would not write it. "Do you want to do a 'call for help'?" I asked. He nodded and then addressed John, a student sitting at one of the tables near him. "Is it a small or capital 'e'?" he mumbled. Once he learned it was capital 'e,' he wrote the rest of the title, making no mistakes. I had a conversation with Pedro after class. Students in middle school were supposed to know that titles were capitalized. What I discovered that day started me on a quest for knowledge on multilingualism, and it changed my life in many ways.

Pedro's parents spoke Spanish at home and lived in a bilingual community. He had been an "English learner" at school from kindergarten—the year he arrived in the country—until fourth grade. His parents had opted out of the bilingual program, so his academic life was entirely in English. At home, nevertheless, there were Spanish newspapers and magazines, and some of the businesses in the community, as well as the local church—Saint Gabriel—had Spanish ads posted on their doors. During our conversation, Pedro explained that he "knew" the English rule, but when it was time to write, "cables would switch" and he had to guess. That day, in class, he had chosen not to guess because there was too much at risk: showing that he was not *as good*. "Can you give me a 'trick' to remember, so next time I know how it should be?" he asked.

English follows one rule, and Spanish, another. Somewhere in Pedro's brain, there was an image of Spanish titles where only the first letter of the first word in a title was capitalized. It was 2005 and I was a young teacher and department supervisor. That day marked the beginning of a path where one answer led to yet another question: *What happens in students' minds when they juggle more than one language and receive explicit instruction only in one? Can they be successful if they see themselves as constant guessers? What can English monolingual teachers do to help students clarify language confusions, and set them on a path towards language mastery and a positive self-image as learners?*

I ended up creating a "trick" or strategy with Pedro. He chose a color for English and one for Spanish—blue and green respectively—and said that those were easy colors to remember because of their association to the flags and the landscapes; it did not matter how much sense it made to me, as long as it did to him. We then reviewed that in English, the *blue* language, since it had two tall letters 'b' and 'l' for blue, first letters of *all* (main) words in titles would be capitalized. The strategy worked for him.

Pedro and I continued to use the color association for other *dual-language* or "translanguaging" moments. From that day onward, translanguaging became our approach: We removed the webs and explored sealed 'brain caves' where both languages had been left entangled; we organized our "blue" and "green" uses into structured linguistic maps. I was not surprised to hear that Pedro began to do better in general, at school. Teachers reported that he was more self-confident and willing to take risks. I could see the change in my class as well. Pedro started to see himself as a good learner, and thus a good student, with the added value of a second language and culture.

Pedro's story is not unique and it does not pertain to language alone. It touches on the need to accept our whole self: not only our complete linguistic repertoire, but also everything else our subcultures imply. Pedro's parents might have opted him out of learning both languages, but he still lives in a bilingual and bicultural world, by virtue of his past. Through explicit instruction in both languages, where both are integrated as one communication system, Pedro—like many of my students—gained language proficiency in both. Students' opportunity to explicitly bring language systems together—to cooperate and make meaning—helps them improve literacy in both languages, and not have to guess any longer, which has a direct impact on how they see themselves in their school and outside of the school community. Furthermore, when educators encourage this integration, students open themselves to contributing to the mainstream community; *since you accept me (and my family) as we are, we accept you.* This is true acculturation and the healthiest way to coexist in a country made up of immigrants—like the United States, and like most countries in the world. The opposite is also true: if we approach their home language or dialect and culture as "the wrong" way, they will not see themselves as part of the larger community—and hence, the creation of *ghettos* in our cities where individuals choose isolation.

Today, most of my research has to do with the effect that identity has on language learning, and the role power and language prestige plays in the shaping of underprivileged students' identity—plus its consequence on academic success, and beyond. I am humbled by my constant discoveries and how much more we need to learn in this regard.

As I reflected on Pedro and the Pedros in my classrooms throughout the years, and what has helped them acculturate, I also reflected on my life. The three Elenas have since merged into one person who is a Mexican-American immigrant, born as a privileged daughter of Andres and Pilar, and a former member of a teaching order that functioned as a cult. An Elena that, today, is that and more—because I am a mother, a friend, and a crazy nature-lover and passionate professor, committed to teacher preparation… And the list doesn't stop here, because identity is not stagnant; it is ever changing.

Chapter 20

ADVOCATE

"The Silent Wars of the Abandoned" is the title I gave to a research project I did on institutionalized children in Mexico. The knowledge I learned in the process added to my identity, because I became an advocate for these children—for life.

My interest in this topic came from my personal experience. In 2009, William and I began the process of becoming parents to two children who were in Mexican institutions, deprived of a family—Joseph, who was seven months old, and Sandra, who was a year older. Their story highlights the tragedy of an unfair system. Joseph was born with serious physical challenges, and he was struggling to stay alive. We adopted Joe but could not adopt Sandra because even though she was "technically" an adoption case, her paperwork was in another state where a new government had been introduced and the process had been delayed. Despite the existence of a law declaring that all Mexican children have the right to grow up in a family, there were still no practices in place to foster children. Therefore, even though Sandra had the legal right to come home, by law, we had to leave her in the orphanage. Two children with similar backgrounds and the same alleged rights, but two very different destinies: one came home before the age of one; the other remained institutionalized until she was almost six. Throughout all those crucial developmental years—while our son was showered with love, received early education intervention, a goodnight kiss, and a bedtime story every day, my daughter navigated dorm life, schooling, and playtime by herself, among about 30 other toddlers.

Years later, when I finally had the opportunity to conduct research on this topic, I realized that there were at least 30,000 children living in Mexican institutions. I tried to understand who they were, and why they were there. *How did Mexico come to have all those children—including Joe and Sandy—institutionalized? And how—despite plentiful laws, and the ceaseless work of heroic individuals both in governmental and nonprofit sectors—has the situation remained almost the same for half a century?* As I concluded my study, I was able to narrow down the single, most significant factor keeping Mexico from making progress in the areas of adoption and foster home placements: bureaucracy.

By the 1960s, the Mexican government—echoing the United Nations' International Covenant on Political Rights—established the system Mexico currently has, where a government entity supervises and directs all issues pertaining children's rights. This organism is called Integral Development of the Family, also referred to as the DIF. The DIF is partisan, so the federal and state elected governments appoint its members at least every six years.

Since then, there have been numerous international treaties and national and state laws declaring that children have rights, and that these are independent from adults' rights. Mexican laws clearly state that it is in all children's best interest to remain with their blood family. In fact, the 2017 amendment made to the 2010 Mexican Law on Children's Rights declared that institutionalization is a temporary solution and it should be the last recourse. It also stipulated that states should create a children's protection committee, which is headed by states' elected governors, their spouses (who automatically become the DIF's presidents), and a governors' appointee general attorney, referred to as *el Procurador.*

As part of my study, I cross-referenced information from three general sources: Mexico's set of laws on children's rights published since 1966; empirical studies and data collection regarding the institutionalization of children in Mexico; and, information from personal conversations I had with DIF representatives and directors of nonprofit institutions.

In the literature I reviewed, the institutions are described as boarding homes or shelters where children reside. Government officials or nonprofits run them, and they are responsible for the care or guardianship of their institutionalized minors. For most of these children, their parents, or a family member, are still their guardians. When that is not the case, it is the state that takes on the guardianship role. Though the buildings are also called *casas hogar,* most of them, far from being *un hogar* (a home), are typically institutions where dozens or hundreds of children of all ages navigate dorm life, schooling, and playtime by themselves. Government funding sponsors the public institutions. The nonprofits—which are the majority—are mostly funded by charitable donations; however, they are still expected to be entirely under the jurisdiction of the DIF, that is, the transient elected government.

Many obstacles prevent institutionalized children from returning to their family or extended family of origin; namely, the family's inability to go through rehabilitation or the intransient condition of vulnerability the family experiences, mainly due to extreme poverty. In addition, and paradoxically, another element that delays the exit of institutionalized children is a law promulgated to protect them. This law declares that the family of origin in Mexico includes the fourth cousins. While the law makes sense in regions where extended family remains together—typically small villages—in urban settings, it prevents children's prompt readmission into a family. This is the case especially because already overwhelmed governors' appointees—the *procuradores*—who might spend the first years of their six-year assignment figuring out the system, need to search the world for children's fourth cousins. Later, such searches and most of the work are interrupted about a year before the end of their term.

The following is a real-life scenario that happened in November of 2017, as recounted by one of the nonprofit directors during our conversation. It illustrates the nonsense of some policies' applications.

A young woman, an orphan and a prostitute—whom I will call Lety—gets pregnant and decides to place her baby girl for adoption through one of the accredited nonprofit institutions. An aunt hears about it and claims the baby. Lety spends all her savings on lawyers, attempting to demonstrate that her aunt is not fit to adopt her baby. In fact, she is the reason why Lety became a prostitute since she sold her at the age of 14. Lety wins the case, but then the *Procurador* turns to the grandmother as a potential adoptive mother. No one realizes that the grandmother is the same woman who turned the other way when Lety was sold. Lety ends up running away with the baby, becoming another vulnerable young mother who might no be able to break away from the vicious cycle of poverty in the country.

I also came across the story of Fernando. He was five when the police found him in the street sitting next to his very drunk mother. He was institutionalized for two months, until the authorities got a hold of his father. The father took him in, but then gave him back to the mother. A year later, the authorities found Fernando again in the same street, sitting next to his intoxicated mother. After another several months of institutionalization, he was taken to his elderly grandmother; but three months later, the grandmother brought Fernando back to the authorities because she was unable to care for him. The authorities then called a great-aunt, who took Fernando in for two more months, but unable to deal with the mother's aggression, the great-aunt brought him back to the institution. Fernando stayed there for a year before he was technically classified as a minor-at-risk and could be transferred to another institution. That year, more than four years since the police first found him in the street, his mother lost custody, so he was sent to a nonprofit institution that would find the funding to provide him with rehabilitation and a family. Fernando is now 10. After suffering negligence and abuse during the fist five years of his life, he spent the following five years with four different relatives who ended up rejecting him, and in three different institutions. After the nonprofit institution found a suitable adoptive family, it took months for state officials to certify the family, and several more months for the courts to process the adoption. Fernando is finally adopted and joined his adoptive family when he was 11— six years after his birth parents first demonstrated their inability to care for him.

Just like Fernando, and my Sandra, approximately 7 percent of Mexican institutionalized children are eventually adopted. An estimated 27 percent leave the institution when they turn 18, and a majority exit during their early teens when they are expected to return "home" in order to start earning money. I can't help but wonder if these are the kids later become the targets of drug cartels or human trafficking.

Though the ideal solution to this situation is the rehabilitation of the families of origin, it is evident that no country will have the infrastructure to effectively rehabilitate all families of origin, and that they cannot wait until this happens to reinstate children in families. But far from being a hopeless situation, it does have a one-step solution: the Mexican Senate could make the bold move to declare a change in the lines of governance that directly oversee and promote the application of children's rights in Mexico. Their Congress lacks a stable government infrastructure to remain in charge of the protection of children's rights when new state governors are elected. The transitional, partisan appointees—because of their temporary role—create a leading and supervisory infrastructure that serves as a shackle with weights attached to a movement of heroic professionals and public and civil servants.

When we adopted Joe, in 2009, the United States had just signed the Hague Convention Treaty, specifying that only Hague-certified US agencies could mediate the adoption process with another Hague Convention country— hence, with Mexico. Since we were US residents, we contacted the only three US agencies that were certified at the time, and all three gave us the same answer: "We do not deal with

Mexico… because it is a mess." My answer to that is: Mexico is not a mess. At least in this field, its people and its institutions are not a mess. It is the thirst for power that keeps the defense of children "a mess." The obstinacy to keep the system under the clutches of elected government officials is what is keeping Mexico from making true progress in the area of adoption and foster home placements. In the meantime, children who deserve it all –like Joe and Sandra, Fernando, and Lety's baby— are deprived of a family—which is meant to be the catalyst of most other gifts.

It is indeed a silent war because children who are institutionalized are taught to rise in the morning and thank God for their food and shelter. However, deep down they know they deserve more than that. And in the silence of their hearts, they fight against themselves—against the fantastic stories with happy endings that they play in their imagination over and over again, of a family to which they belong; and they fight against their fear that one day they will stop deserving or remembering that they deserve.

People like me never forget what institutionalized children *deserve*, because we live with reminders. I have two of them at home.

Chapter 21

MOTHER

We have raised the kids with a sense of gratitude and love towards their birth mothers, for giving them the opportunity to live, to love and be loved. I write to Joe' birth mother every year on his birthday, and since both adoptions were closed adoptions, I pray that one day I can give her all those letters. Sandy's mom is already in heaven.

This sense of gratitude towards their birth mothers did not come spontaneously. I learned it partly from a friend. Having been adopted himself, he looked for his birth mother when he was an adult, to thank her for giving birth to him. I also learned it from one of the hardest experiences I lived before we adopted Joe and Sandy. It was 2007, and a friend referred us to an unwed mother who wished to give her unborn baby girl up for adoption. The following week, when we contacted our friend to begin the legal adoption process, she informed us that the unwed mom had changed her mind and was thinking about terminating the pregnancy. We pleaded to keep the baby, and even began getting ready for a court appearance in the hope that a family judge would rule in favor of letting the baby live and be adopted. We never got to that point. The next time we contacted our friend, the woman had aborted the baby girl. I still cry when I think about her. I will never hug her or make her laugh; she was forever gone, before she could experience love.

One of the main lessons I have learned as adoptive mother, and maybe the lesson all mothers learn, is that our main role is to help our children understand that our love for them was, is, and will always be. Children who were adopted can tend to think that they were abandoned, even when it was the opposite of abandonment what led their birth mothers to place them for adoption. This leads many of them to test the love of their adoptive mother, actively seeking their abandonment... before their attachment grows and thus becomes vulnerable.

I remember a day when I had meticulously prepared the kids their lunch for school. On our way to school, Sandra took a mustard filled bread slice and smeared it in the back of the passenger seat, dumping the sandwiches' contents on the car floor... not as part of a tantrum, but just "because." We had had a wonderful and fun weekend together, where she and I had bonded. On Monday morning, when the sentiments of attachment towards me sank in, she decided she needed to do something—anything—that would push me away... before the love would grow and with it, the pain of a potential second abandonment. Instead, before dropping her off, I gave her a hug and said: "I am sad that you might be hungry later. I love you and I will always love you." She was only seven and gave me an adult-like smirk, which turned into a genuine smile, and then it reached her eyes. She turned and left. "You are stuck with my love!" I yelled through the window as she walked away. As I left in the car, I noticed she was still smiling.

As a mother, my identity is to make sure they know that "they are stuck with my love," and with what my absolute love implies.

~~~

I am spending the night at a seminary where teen boys are being trained to become priests in the future... I can endure the pain of remaining there some more hours, some more days... It is dark and everyone is asleep. I walk up the stairs; Maciel is visiting but I will not be called into his room. While in the minor seminary, he calls the younger ones. I enter a dormitory; the beds are small, a child sleeps soundly on each. I approach one that is empty. A label on the headboard reads: Joseph. No.... "Where is my baby, Joe?!" Little Joey just turned eight. "No! Not my Joe! I have to get him out of here immediately, I have to find him before Maciel gets to him too!"

I woke up and sat at my desk. I looked among my computer files for the book I started to write after my divorce. This time, I thought, I will complete it and make my story known. I realize that what I wouldn't do for myself when I was young—flee and alert others—I would do for my children and other children. Parents need to learn to recognize abusive narcissists, and abusive systems. And so, I wrote…

Chapter 22

ONGOING BEGINNINGS

Because I believe in a God who is also wise and powerful, even when the temptation to hate myself comes along, I experience a sense that my existence is worth every trial and that I am immensely lovable; otherwise, why would a loving, powerful, and wise God create me? This conviction kept me optimistic and excited about every stage in life... The awareness that there is—still—a gift waiting behind every door I open, is exciting. Even in RC—despite the emotional and psychological abuses I endured—I received wonderful gifts (like the gift of learning to teach, to meditate, and to appreciate good people, and to value every comfort in life). In my marriage, I received the gift of my two wonderful children, to whom both of us—their father and I—remain totally committed.

During my years in RC, I learned to pretend I was OK. We were taught that certain dishonesty is justified with a "greater end in mind." Teresa, my childhood friend—the one who had and rode horses in her backyard, also joined the consecrated branch of RC. She and I coincided in Rome during our formation years. One day, superiors asked her to lie to Italian agents working for Motor Vehicles regarding the whereabouts of a car. The goal was to fake the car's "death" so as to avoid the tedious Italian paperwork and, in so doing, avoid paying taxes. RC's vehicles in Rome had fake foreign license plates... so the cars wouldn't be registered in Italy. But the car she lied about was donated by an Italian family and therefore had been registered. And so, she arrived to the Motor Vehicles' counter and told the agent that the car was totaled in a terrible accident. After taking care of some signatures and paper work, she left, but not before stopping at the bathroom to throw up, so disgusted with herself for the lie. For several months, every day, when she would see the allegedly dead car still traversing the streets of Rome and arriving to sleep in our garage, she regretted lying. Until, finally, she got used to seeing the zombie car in broad daylight... calling her a liar.

In the same way Teresa was asked to lie in the name of God, I was told to pretend to be OK, and I complied because maybe I was OK. We were taught that as long as we were fulfilling God's will, expressed through directors' commands and wishes, we were OK... And if we remained unhappy, it was simply because "the flesh is weak," and our selfishness protests. Throughout my 10 years of marriage, which immediately followed my departure from RC, I also pretended to be OK, because maybe I was OK. I thought I was doing everything I was expected to do as a wife. I did not experience the fulfillment of love during those years, but then, RC taught me human love was not supposed to satisfy me, since "only God satisfies and suffices." My children and friendships—including my current romantic relationship—however, taught me the opposite. In the same way that Joe taught me to love and fight for a joyful life, Sandra taught me to fight for my God-given rights. It was in fighting for her rights that I was inspired to fight for mine.

Had I not joined a religious sect, I probably would have thought that everyone who joins a sect is weak, needy, or stupid. The same can happen with divorce. Had I not gone through divorce with two young children, I would have thought that everyone who gets a divorce in those circumstances is selfish... Actually, the opposite can be true.

In 2014, we sold our apartment in Bronxville, New York, and moved into two different homes in central Connecticut. Since the move was in the summer and I was still working for New Rochelle school district, I commuted to work for one more year. After that, I accepted a job offer as a Languages Supervisor in a Connecticut school district. Since William lived a mile from my condo, we were able to organize our parenting schedule in such a way that the kids could have both of us as much as possible.

William and I received the annulment of our Catholic marriage on the grounds that we had gotten married when I was out of an abusive institution for only a year and, thus, I was not emotionally and psychologically fit to marry. I cried and rejoiced the afternoon I received the letter from the Archdiocese of Hartford. The tears came from realizing that I was still the black bird who was deceived and deceived others; I had delayed for so many years a healing process that should have started immediately after leaving RC. My tears of joy came from acknowledging that it is never too late for a new beginning.

It was during my second year in Connecticut—during the first week of a new school year—that I heard about the tragic accident and death of an acquaintance that had been the Director of Religious Education in our parish. Her name was Ava, she was only 48 and had a husband and two children, one entering middle school, and another going into high school. As it is the district's custom, I reached out to the parent —Ava's widower—Edward, to extend my condolences and reassure him that our teachers would assist his kids to catch up with any schoolwork they might miss due to their initial grieving period.

Ava's death was a tragedy and an extremely sad event. One sunny Sunday in the summer, she left for a bike ride; a few days later, only her ashes came back home. It changed Edward's life forever. I didn't know, at that point, the extent to which that tragedy would change my life as well.

Chapter 23

DEATH
…Is not the opposite of life, but part of it

I walked into Sedgwick middle school after a long trip from Baja California, Mexico. I had scheduled my return flight—from one of my niece's weddings—to arrive just on time for the middle school parent-teacher fall meeting. As I entered the building and turned towards one of the hallways where I expected to see most of the 6th grade parents, I saw him. His silhouette stood out—to me—as if he were the only gray image transported from an old picture into a colorful scenery of adults laughing and talking. We were at opposite ends of the hallway, and yet, I felt I could hear his fast breathing, and could sense his effort to contain the tears. I was immediately impelled to be near him before the dam of tears would open; I knew I had few chances to make it to the end of the hallway on time.

I should have been stopped on the way to him either by a parent, a teacher, or by a fellow supervisor. Instead, the voices and the shapes of people in the hallway became blurry, and—as I approached him—the man at the end became clearer, until his voice was the only one I could hear.

"Hi."

"Hi."

"–You ok? Can I be of any help?"

It took that short question for Edward's tears to get loose and roll down his cheeks.

"I'm not sure what I am supposed to do. Ava always did–" He could not finish the sentence.

"Have you met Christa's Chinese teacher?" I asked him.

"Do you know that Ava spoke some Chinese? She is—was—so good with languages. She always encouraged the kids to learn languages. She lived in Taiwan… and when we were in Cape Verde—we were there with Peace Corp for two years—she picked up Portuguese right away…"

I let him speak about his deceased love until it was almost time to gather for a general session in the school's auditorium.

Something that I still cannot explain led me to notice Edward that night. Three days later, the same happened at Conard High School where Steve—his son—was starting 9th grade. This time, he came into my office and we spoke. I tried to convey to him some important school information, knowing that he was probably in a daze and none of it would seem as important as the fact that Ava was no longer with us, had not attended the meetings, and would never come back to attend school meetings… or anything else… ever.

Death is absolutely finite, and it is part of life.

The next time Edward and I communicated, I found myself proposing we go out for a non-date beer, outside of town, where no one knew us and no one would judge us. We both needed non-committal company on the days our kids were out with friends or other activities, and our homes felt empty.

Chapter 24

I Can Cook

Edward put the fork back on the plate. And looked out the window as he savored the food. I looked at him intently, unable to taste my food yet.

"Well?" I asked.

"My... I don't know why you say you don't cook."

"Because I don't... I mean I do, but I'm not good at it," I replied.

"This is delicious," he said before he took another bite, which he seemed to enjoy. Then he asked: "Is it important for you to be able to cook?"

"Yes, of course," I said.

"Well, you know what they say: 'If you can read, you can cook.'"

I could surely read, but I had never been able to cook. I did not learn to cook early in life.

"Really? You really like it?" I was still incredulous.

"I do. It's very good!"

I had prepared a dish of Parmesan chicken and potatoes. It was my first time preparing an actual dish that did not imply frying eggs, grilling steak, or tossing a salad.

"I can cook, then!" I said, an immense grin on my face. "I can cook!" I repeated.

"Of course you can. Why wouldn't you be able to cook?"

"I don't know... cooking is... was... not *my thing*."

Edward looked at me with a mixture of tenderness, affection and, probably, compassion. "Anything you want to do—or you consider important for you to do—*is* your thing."

"You think so?"

"Of course," he said with a smile that I had only seen on him... a mixture of affection, care, and amusement. "Tell me something you want to do and you can't because it is 'not *your thing.*'"

I stopped to reflect for a moment... There were so many. I considered Edward's question while he got up to grab two beers from the refrigerator. I wanted to be a fun mom, and not just a breadwinning driver and homework tutor. I wanted to learn tap dancing and hip-hop, to go camping and bird watching, to research important topics and write books, to study a doctoral degree and be a professor. I wanted to be a good investor and buy a home with beautiful mountain or ocean views. I wanted to ride horses again, to own a dog... I thought of Ricky and Lucy with sadness; they were long gone, but not before I had to place them with a family friend because the apartment where William and I lived in Manhattan, after we got married, wouldn't accept dogs. I still couldn't remember how that had happened... how I had agreed to live there.

"Uhh...where do I start?" I said as I took a sip of beer.

"Why? Are there many?" he said still with a smile.

Edward's eyes are blue... not any blue; they are *kind and peaceful* blue, and when he smiles, they smile too. I wanted to reach out and grab his hand affectionately to thank him for being so good to me. But we were just friends and a gesture like that could be misunderstood. Ava had died earlier that year, and friends was all we could be for the moment—good friends. We were in my condo, and I had invited him for dinner. We had turned Saturday nights, every other week, into our "support group." We had intended to invite everyone we knew who was too sad to be home alone on Saturday nights... but the last few times, it had been just the two of us.

I didn't want to scare him so I chose only one "desire" that I did not do because it was not *my thing*: "I want to learn tap dancing and hip-hop," I finally said.

"And..."

"And, what?"

"Why don't you?" he asked.

When I met Edward, I knew I wanted to be his friend for life... I had met Ava briefly at church. Later, after her passing, Edward and I had a work relationship: his children attended two of the schools where I supervised languages. But during our first non-work encounter, when he and I met for a non-date beer, I experienced what I have felt only a few times in life: a sense that I was home.

The following week, I interviewed with a dance teacher at a studio near my house.

"I only teach one adult tap class; it is an advanced class. Have you taken tap before?" she asked.

I heard myself saying: "Yes." I hadn't but I had tap-danced a bit during a musical, in high school where I had mainly done jazz. I presumed it could count.

But then the teacher asked, "For how many years?"

Is it OK to say a white lie? I justified it by telling myself that I was a fast learner. "Uhh.. I danced several years." I was careful not to say what type of dance...

"Tuesdays at 7 pm; see you tomorrow... We can decide then if you are ready for that."

I asked her if I could record the dance and start the following week so I could have time to practice it and catch up. She agreed and I left. I had to stop myself from skipping all the way to my car.

The class had been in session for months and dancers were preparing for a public performance in May. I arrived before the class was over and I recorded the dance—3 minutes of intense tap, with steps I had never done in my life. *Tap was not my thing...* Someone had discouraged me from dancing tap some years back... because it is not something you pick up "at my age."

I spent over 10 hours that week looking at tap-dancing videos, practicing steps, and learning the dance I was supposed to perform in three months. And when I showed up in class the following Tuesday, I blended in. I could tap dance! Just like that, tap dancing became *my thing*.

I did the same with hip-hop the following week.

When I told Edward what I had done, he gave me an affectionate bear hug, and then we laughed together. How many other things had I excluded from my life because they were not *my thing?*

A few months later, I performed in an enormous auditorium, at Connecticut Central State University. I tap danced—with a dozen younger women—to the tune of "Shut Up and Dance with Me," wearing a black top hat and short tailcoat.

Within the following two years, it was not only cooking and tap dancing that became my thing. I also performed a fun dance with my daughter during International Night, at her school, I took the kids camping, I got a dog, and I began my search for a small beachfront or mountain view property. I also began my doctoral degree in Curriculum and Instruction with a specialization in Multilingual and Multicultural Education at the University of Connecticut; and I wrote and presented my first two research papers. Many more things became *my thing,* because they became part of how I envisioned my life; it was part of what we call, in my area of research, my "imagined identity," or as Pamela—a friend—says: *Cuando no conozcas tu futuro, invéntalo a tu ventaja* (when you do not know your future, make it up to your advantage).

That summer, a year after Ava's passing, it became harder to hide my romantic feelings for Edward. I was aware he was still in his grieving and dazed stage—which would probably last for months if not years—and I was determined to brace myself for what I thought would be a long and bittersweet wait. It had been three years for me, but only one for him.

~ ~ ~ ~

The rifle is aiming straight at me. I am on the grounds of what seems to be a university. Its buildings are stately, and the facades are covered with red brick and stone. There are porches with white tall pillars... It could be Yale... it could be Harvard. I know it is useless to run. I will probably be shot. I choose to try... it is the only option I have, and so I run for my life. Only a minute or two before, I was speaking to the woman in charge of keeping me safe... some sort of security bodyguard. Is she also the director of the center where I live? Am I back in RC? The woman in charge, my bodyguard, had delineated a perfect plan to keep me alive. We had just gone over it together. Yet, somehow, I am still in danger of being shot. I fear that sooner or later, I will be in the killer's sights...

And that moment arrives; it is here and it is now. My heartbeat accelerates, and without losing sight of the rifle clearly pointing at me, I run as fast as my heavy feet allow me towards the only object that can protect me: a pecan tree. I recognize the tree. It was there when I was a girl; I would sit by it when I was sad... mostly when my parents had left for a trip. No one seems to notice or mind the man standing in the middle of the lawn, holding the rifle pointing at me...in broad daylight. Am I the only one who can see I will die? My legs cannot move. I feel an urge to save the women around me, including the one that, ironically, was supposed to protect me. And so, as I scream, "Everyone to the ground!" I hear a shot and I wake up in panic.

I could recognize the type of dream very well. I had learned to see it as a sign. It never failed. While in RC, when my psychology would reach its limits of endurance, my subconscious always knew it first, and would create a dream where I was being killed or almost killed. They were like anonymous tips, like the riddle of an elf that lived in my soul, which I was suppose to decipher before it was too late. Sometimes the dream would carry on for days, or even weeks, until I would listen and transfer my emotional stress from the subconscious to a more accessible consciousness. The places, the people, and the weapons or circumstances would change, but it was always the same: I was going to die. The same happened during my last years of my marriage. It had become obvious to me that the danger was mainly emotional. Thank God for an assertive subconscious... or a mischievous, though smart and tenacious elf who anticipated the danger and would tell me about it in riddles he would repeat for weeks at a time. But... why was I identifying my present moment with that tortuous period in my life? The elf had anticipated danger and was warning me. It was time to accept that my relationship with Edward was making me vulnerable again. Like in the past, I could be totally conditioned to the reactions of a man. *No! Never... I can never go back to that.* I knew that somehow I had to learn to love without giving up my conscience, my judgment, and my heart. Even while in love with Edward, I needed to belong to myself.

Chapter 25

THE VALUE OF PATIENCE

Around the time my marriage annulment came through, a few years after the legal divorce, I was happy to know that my feelings for Edward were reciprocated. However, far from making the relationship easier, the awareness of our mutual growing love made it quite complicated. We were a middle-aged man and woman, with four pre-teen and teen children, living in two different homes, with two dogs, and four extended families. He had a full time job as a data analyst, and I was a full-time doctoral candidate with a part-time job at the University of Connecticut. Though we were honest with our children and told them about our intentions, we soon realized they were not interested in changing anything about their lives.

"At least it means that the kids are happy with their lives as they are," Edward said. He was standing in his house kitchen, resting his back against the counter. Dinner was in the oven.

"In a way, I don't want to change anything either. I have a perfect life," I said provokingly with a smile, knowing that his life was still a bit in chaos.

He approached me with a smirk and—after turning around to make sure the kids were not around—he held both of my hands. "I don't think your life is quite perfect yet." I had to guess he was referring to the lack of intimacy—the certain celibacy—we were forced into. We smiled. "Are you suggesting we abstain from intimacy for the next nine years?" he whispered.

Joe, the youngest, was in 4th grade and wouldn't leave for college—if he chose to do so—for another eight years.

"No–" I barely answered as I cleared my throat. Edward kept smiling. I was nervous. "You are having fun with this!" I told him. My nervousness started to turn into frustration. I gently let go of his hands and walked to get a glass of water. I looked at the window and the backyard. Edward's home was a beautifully kept, three-room Colonial home, with a large deck and garden.

"I'm sorry... I truly am. I need time, my kids need time," he said.

I knew they did. I knew it all along. The fact that our growing love was mutual did not change our circumstances. The paradox was that I had just discovered—partially, thanks to Edward—that I was my future's author, but I could not change my future with Edward. The fact that I could only control what *I* did sank in.

"No need to apologize," I said, still whispering... the kids could show up any minute.

By the time dinner was ready, the kitchen was spotless and I remained scrubbing a clean sink. I turned the faucet off and dried my hands, still standing by the sink. I rested the front of my hip on the counter and looked outside. Edward's deck was almost orange, a color that neither he, nor the kids liked. I didn't like it either. He hired a man to treat it and paint it shortly after Ava's accident, and he had not supervised the work as closely as he usually supervises house chores. He blamed himself for it for a few days, until he decided he would turn it into a life-lesson: moving forward, "an orange-deck moment" would refer to moments that should be avoided thanks to the practice of patience, prudence, and careful consideration.

I understood him perfectly. I had a different title for similar moments; for me, it was "the-piano-and-the-scratch moment." When I first moved into my condo, I decided I could move furniture around by myself, including a 300-pound piano my kids' sitter had given me. Impatient to see the results and not wanting to wait, I moved the piano from one wall to another across the living room. As a result I got a scratch on the floor that shows with the reflection of the light coming from the sliding door that opens to my deck. I see the scratch every time

I come home. After lamenting my impatience for days, I had also decided to turn it into a "the-piano-and-the-scratch moment;" something to remind me that I should not rush into anything again.

I smiled, looking at the ugly orange on the deck. The fact that destiny had granted us both reminders that would "show up" every day at home was definitively "a sign," or a "voice in our conscience" to which we should listen. Even though Edward and I live without a bucket list, aware that life is short, we still did not rush into marriage, or into merging our families. Instead, we began our second teenage stage in life, where we had to hide to *kiss*. This time we were not hiding from our parents, but rather from our kids. Mine were still at that stage when a kiss is gross, and his were mourning the loss of the only woman they had ever seen their dad kiss.

I read quite a bit about how to help others grieve for the loss of loved ones. It became evident that I needed to have a conversation with Edward's children, and so I did.

"I will never replace your mom... I will never try to replace her because I can't. Your mom is in heaven, and will always be your mom," I told Christa as we were driving back from a successful shopping trip to the mall.

"I know."

"What I would very much like to be is your friend."

"OK," Christa replied with a smile. At 13, she was as tall as me—almost 5'8. Though she looks more like Ava, she has Edward's sweet and smiley eyes. "You should stay home when you drop me off and watch a movie with us. How about *The Sound of Music*?" she added.

I smiled, "Perfect. I love that movie."

I soon learned to love Christa and Steve, and because I love them, I made sure to make room for their angel mom in their lives. For Steve's confirmation present, I gave him a locket photo keychain—aware that we might not have need for them in a constantly digitalized world. I felt it was important to engrave "Forever with You," and place Ava's photo inside. I had given Sandra one for her 11th birthday—a necklace, with "Love You" engraved and a photo of her birth mother with her, taken when she was months old. "You need to remember that you were forever loved, Steph," I said when I gave it to her.

~ ~ ~ ~

The Sound of Music is shown on a large TV screen. Novice Maria... Julie Andrews... is in a dark room with walls of stone. Across from her, sitting on a large chair, is an older woman... Mother Superior. They were engaged in a conversation. "You will not love God any less for loving a man, Maria."

In the next scene, Novice Maria, now freed from her convent outfit... and from all outfits, was with a coronel, kissing or getting married... the scenes were overlapping fast.

When I became aware of my dream, I smiled. It was such a corny and beautiful movie. I had seen it in my teens... After that, I never saw it since it was not one of the "approved movies" in RC. I had questioned it when I was in the movement; it seemed such a pure and faith-filled story. It is not approved because "the novice leaves the order and gets married, living happily ever after, which doesn't happen in real life," I was told when I asked the director about it. As I watched it again, with Christa and Edward, I had realized it contradicted one of Maciel's teachings. Maciel had taught that the love for a man or woman in a romantic form or even in a friendship takes away from our love for God. In the movie, Mother Superior tells Maria, the novice who has fallen in love, exactly the opposite: "You will not love God less for loving a man." *Damn, Maciel.* How can one love God less for loving a man? But then, Maciel—being an abusive narcissist—needed to undermine human relationships; it is what narcissists do due to their acute cynicism and their incapacity to love.

My growing affection for Edward wouldn't lead me to love God less. On the other hand, avoiding Edward's love out of fear of loving God less, could lead me to lose both... out of bitterness.

God, I thank you for life, I love you and I need you. Help me to heal and understand the value of patience in "living the life I intend to live."

Chapter 26

WORDS ARE NOT JUST WORDS

We tend to underestimate the power that language has within us and around us. One of my favorite studies is Lev Vygotsky's book, *Thought and Language*, where he develops the theory that *these* are inseparable. Thought and language happen within the human brain, in a seesaw motion that leads to understanding and creating concepts. At the same time inner-speech happens in a child, a concept is also attached to that speech—a word or set of words—and with that action emerges more abstract thinking. Subsequently, the thinking looks for words and—again—moves it forward toward more sophisticated thinking... which provokes vocabulary expansion. In other words, both—thought and language—are part of a whole; either one, by itself, cannot create concepts.

When we have politicians using certain rhetoric or language, their PR professionals cannot excuse them by saying it was *just* the wrong choice of words. As researched by Vygotsky and many others, words come with thoughts and these reveal the person's concepts. Eventually, words create an imagined identity, community, and culture; hence, politicians' responsibility to "choose" words that enable a harmonious culture—one where harmony, like in music, is produced by differences in its members.

As I live no other life but "the life I intend to live," I have delved into the language that reflects my thinking about the different situations in my life. While I did not intend to be recruited by an abusive narcissist and I did not intend to "adore" him, it did happen, and it is my responsibility to understand the process and learn from it, giving this new *understanding* adequate *language*, Vygotsky style. Many of the conversation I have had with kind and intelligent people—like Edward and others—have helped me advance this thinking, and to reframe those events in my life.

"So what happened? How can the Legion and RC be so successful if it had such a horrible founder and leader?" Laura asked.

Edward and I had decided to participate, with the children, in a family weekend retreat at the Monastery and Retreat Center in our town. Laura was one of the organizers and an articulate and bright Notre Dame graduate. The children had gone to rest and the adults were getting ready to play Apple to Apples in one of the Center's lounges.

It was a question I asked myself many times. By the time the founder died, the Legion and RC were worth about 650 million dollars and 1 billion in assets—including hundreds of successful schools and three universities (according to a February 18, 2013, NCR article). Before, when someone asked the question Laura had just asked, I would play a trailer in my head where the narrator said with a low and loud voice: *Yes! He fooled thousands of people around the world, forced them into hard labor, and gave himself the life of a lazy maharani.* But little by little, I started to feel more comfortable with the line of questioning.

I exhaled and gave an oblique smile. "Maciel was a pervert, but like many perverts, he was extremely charismatic. He knew what to say, when to say it, who to win over, and who to keep at a distance. He also chose carefully who to abuse sexually, who emotionally, and where to stop. He fooled us all. He also recruited very good people. He never really made himself vulnerable or available to most of us—it was always through others who, fortunately or unfortunately, were *better* than him... He used ambassadors that were genuine... some became as abusive, but the majority of these individuals did not."

"Yes... it's sad. And I can see that happening," Laura said. "Where were you when you joined?"

"In Monterrey, in Mexico."

"And, if you don't mind me asking, why did you join knowing the rules were so tough? It's a pretty strict order, isn't it?" Andrea, another friend and retreat participant, asked.

"I wanted to make a difference. It's a bit of a cliché... but that is what it was. Maciel presented that life to me as the most effective and noble way to do it."

I did not go into details. I could have... but chose not to. As a child, I was spiritual. The first chapter book I ever read was *The Song of Bernadette*, and it left a mark on me. When I was eight, I told my mother I wanted to adopt all the children in Africa that didn't have parents so I could feed them, dress them, and love them. In my naiveté I thought, at the time, that the only reason why children starved was because they did not have parents to feed them. I could have also explained to Laura that I never "heard a calling from God," but that Maciel had told me that I could and should simply offer my life to God, otherwise, I would risk being selfish. And, at 18, I believed him.

"Wow... just like that? And why did you leave the order, then?" Amy—yet another retreat participant—asked.

Edward gave me an empathetic look. *Are you OK?* he seemed to ask.

I smiled at him, and then addressed Amy's question. Some time back, the question would have bothered me. But something had changed. I learned that I had the language to express why I had left because I could finally understand why I had done it. Besides, I owed them an explanation because they were Edward's friends, and my friends. "The order—though it had some wonderful people—got to be saturated by a philosophy and extreme practices established by Maciel, a sick or maybe evil... only God knows... man. Many of the rules he established did away with our inner freedom. I joined young. My family had been involved, so I trusted Maciel by virtue of everyone else that trusted him, and whom I loved. In my 30s, with maturity and God's help, the abuses became evident, and so I left."

Edward's expression had changed. He was listening absorbedly with his hands folded on the table. I decided to wrap it up on a positive note... Shame on me if I were not the carrier of good news! It had been part of my training. I smiled. "Many of us left the order before the Vatican *punished* Maciel, because we got sick. Years later, we realized we had gotten sick because we experienced coercion of freedom and individual judgment. It has taken me time to recover and eradicate some bad self-defeating habits. But overall, I think I took with me many great memories and lessons."

"I can't picture you as a nun," Bill said. Everyone laughed... Bill was a trained actor and a natural comedian, so his comment must have been accompanied by gestures I missed. I looked at Edward for reassurance. He was smiling too... and I smiled: "Yeah, I get that a lot."

After our game and after checking on the kids, I went to bed. Edward went into his room as well.

~ ~ ~ ~

I am in Rome and I find Father Jonas. He is kneeling by an altar dedicated to the Gregorian Madonna, one of the many "small" altars inside Saint Peter's Basilica, in the Vatican. He cries. I feel tremendous relief to see him. Had I been looking for him? "Father Jonas, you must do it!" *I feel angry.* "Even if you are a priest, you must be a father to your son!" *Father Jonas continues to cry; he is kneeling with his hands together holding his chin.*

"Elena, I only want to do God's will and my superiors just told me I had to treat the incident with total discretion."

My irritation grows. "For the love of God, Jonas... the child is not theirs! He is yours! Please Jonas, react." ...*uck, ...uck, ...uck... Is it double sin to curse inside of a church... worse if it is a cathedral? Jonas cries and tumbles to the hard, cold marble floor... I lose my balance trying to hold him... I fall with him.*

I woke up.

I was in a small and plain room. It was the Retreat Center.

Jonas had been a colleague priest in the Legion. To say the man was handsome was an understatement. He was a version of Michelangelo's David with clothes... with priestly clothes. He was also smart and had a great sense of humor... an exemplary man. *He still is.* He had fathered a child with the woman he loved. In reality, the conversation I had with Jonas in my dream never happened, but my subconscious must have kept the desire to tell him that the child came first. Maciel had put the institution first and the Legion and RC adopted that philosophy. A child that was brought into this world by a woman and a man should not lack either. Parenthood is *the* intrinsic sacrament superior to all other sacraments and human mandates... so intrinsic in nature that God did not need to establish it through other forms of revelation.

God, I thank you for my life, I love you, and I need you. Help priests understand that their birth children come first.

As I got out of bed that morning, I made some notes in my journal. While in RC, I lived the life I intended to live... I did not intend the abuses, but I intended the many other good things that I enjoyed while there: meditation, reading, professional preparation, and getting to know outstanding people. While in marriage, I lived the life I intended to live... I did not intend the failure, but I intended to become a mother and love my children with all my heart. I also intended to further my career in New York—which definitively set me up for professional success in the years to come.

Chapter 27

NEXT STEP IN OUR RELATIONSHIP

In life, we are faced with hundreds of small decisions, and many times we don't even realize it. The intentionality of our actions is what defines us as humans. I had gone back to biking, hiking, riding, dancing, skiing. I had forgotten that skiing was such a great exercise. I put to use some muscles I didn't even remember having. The last time I skied, I was 16. It had been a memorable trip since I traveled to Aspen with my parents and my six siblings, including my two older sisters' husbands and toddlers; they each had a son. Since my sisters graduated from high school and married at 19 and 20, shortly after my mom had given birth to her seventh child, my sisters' babies—both boys—were only a few years younger than my little brother. This gave us a family life where there was always a baby being born, with the joy that that brings.

So much in my life had changed when I joined the movement... I had to give up family with its trips, horseback riding with the cousins, water skiing at the *Presa de la Boca* with my brothers, dancing at the *Club Casino*, and playing tennis at the *Campestre Country Club*. I never really liked shopping for clothes, so it was not "a sacrifice" to give that up; I was happy inheriting the clothes any of my three older sisters did not want to wear anymore. Everything had changed when I joined but, then, that is what was expected. Less than 10 percent of the world's population live deprived of all those experiences and they can live happy lives. The problem is not the deficit of things or experiences but rather, the deficit of free will and judgment. People have the right to choose their own priorities in life, with the resources that they can earn or that they have.

After RC and after my marriage, I began to embrace all the activities I love doing—I do many of them with my kids and with friends. My assertiveness was coming back, but not completely. I still had not told Edward how I felt about his choice to wait to merge families until the kids were older.

It was still as if the real me were watching events from the stands, partially absent. The woman with my name, with my face and my body, sitting on the stands needed to come up on stage and claim her role.

"Did you know that there is such a thing as *modern rustic?*"

Edward looked puzzled. "Aha..." he said.

I laughed. I realized that what I was saying did not make sense out of context. "My style... I finally realized what my style is: it is modern rustic."

Finding out and "giving language" to my *preferences*—even unimportant ones—was part of my attempt to regain my complete identity.

"Oh... that's good. Is that a clothing style?"

"Maybe... yes, probably that is also my style in clothing, though I was referring to furniture." I had been living on my own for four years, and the topic would pop into my head like a movie trailer, yet again: *"She submitted... she doesn't know what her style is. When she is asked what type of food she likes, she remains speechless,"* the narrator's voice would say with dramatic music in the background.

We stopped at the top of the hill where we found a bench. Our monthly hikes had become a routine, but we also anticipated them with a sense of suspense—*would a child get sick, would they have a school project that needed supervision?* We never knew if one of our four children would have a particular need that would deter us from our monthly hike or our weekly soirees.

Edward sat down, and since he was still holding my hand, he pulled me towards him, making me fall on his lap. I placed my right arm around his shoulders for stability. I felt so very aware of Edward's body under me and was feeling terribly nervous. Apparently, he was oblivious to my fidgeting.

"So you have a style? And you have a style in men?"

"You." My answer was spontaneous but genuine.

He smiled. "So, what is going on?"

"Is it that obvious?"

"A little bit," he replied.

"I feel like a fish in air," I said.

He smiled again. "I presume a fish in air feels like a fish out of water."

I smiled back as I realized my mistake... I change language expressions often. I do it both in English and in Spanish. Edward calls them "Elenisms." It is common for me to refer to a certain Mrs. White as Mrs. Snow. My siblings used to tease me, saying that my ability to make all sort of linguistic brain connections surpassed that of our paternal grandmother, whose family used to do it constantly. "Brilliant but distracted," my father would explain, in an attempt to reassure me. *Sweet.*

"What do you mean?" Edward asked.

"I am trying to be assertive and become aware of my preferences... fashion and furniture is one thing, but there is something more important. I know we are not rushing into anything major, but sometimes I feel like we have our relationship on hold until our kids grow up... and I don't want that. You more than anyone understand that life is short." Edward, who probably originally thought he could have a good time teasing me, seemed to be worried all of a sudden. I continued: "I am finally over my 'trust issues,' Edward, but then I can't have you because the kids are young... Why?" I added.

"So, what can we do to move our relationship forward?" he asked.

"I don't know... I don't want to get married."

"You don't?"

"I mean not now, not soon... But I do want to spend more time with you–" When I realized what I was saying, I stopped talking. I did not want to give the wrong impression. "Would you think I am needy if I tell you that I feel like a mistress you're hiding, and sometimes I get jealous?" I ventured to ask coyly.

"I like it when you're candid. Besides, I'm pleased. It means you have feelings for me. Why wouldn't I be happy? Besides, I also feel jealous sometimes when jetsetter friends come from other countries to see you... It's hard for me to believe that you are really that clueless, but I am getting used to it... and I want to believe I'm getting better at anticipating your 'confusions.' So, tell me, I won't judge... I'll try to understand and see what we can do about it."

For the first time in a long time, I realized—in a practical way—there was actually an alternative to being judged: provide input, assimilate input, and respond to questions. It was a practice I used in my professional life when I evaluated students or teachers, but not quite in my personal life.

We spoke. We decided we could use some vacation time—the two of us, and also the six of us. Then, amidst laughter, we continued talking about furniture styles. When he said he would count on me for all style decisions, I told him it made me feel empowered. I wasn't sure if he could understand the depth of my comment. In RC, men were the ultimate deciders for... pretty much everything. There was a woman director in each of the centers where "consecrated women" lived, but she responded to a territorial superior male... and men were also the directors of the different areas: apostolate, spirituality, and finances. Even the rules on the dress code and the no-makeup and no-facial-moisturizers rule had been determined by a man... a priest, chosen by Maciel to assist him in the direction of all the women and the coordination of their work, including their assignments. Many times I expressed my concern about the fact that when the hierarchy included only men, but decisions affected women, the organization was doomed to fail. "Female partnership strengthens it and has synergetic results," I used to argue. "It is just like marriage —I suppose—where a husband-father does not oppose a mother's intuition when it's strong." That is the way I remembered it at home.

That day, I took yet another step towards the integration of my identity, where the Elena with the voice came up on stage. This allowed me to move forward in my relationship with Edward. I learned that when I enable the voice in my heart, I move towards the direction I *intend* to go in life.

Chapter 28

DECLUTTERING

Several weeks into my relationship with Edward, I found out he was a Marie Kondo fan. Many around the world consider this woman a decluttering and home-organization guru. I shied away from her books for a while, since one of the perks of having been in a cult is that you tend to be skeptical of people who are admired by the masses. Still, motivated by my need to keep my small office and abundant paperwork organized, I decided to give Kondo a try.

Marie Kondo recommends you should start by organizing items that are less sentimental, while you develop *an ear* for your inner voice. She suggests we ask ourselves the question "Does this spark joy?" and keep only what does and what we use. So after clothing and books, I began with my piles of "personal" papers. When I came across journals, articles, and books from the time I was in RC, I set them aside, since they were at the top of my list of sentimental items; I had absolutely nothing from my childhood because I had either given or thrown everything away when I joined consecrated life. Our promise of poverty implied doing away with all sentimental items from the past.

On one Tuesday night—the only weekday night Edward and I were able to meet by ourselves—he came into my room and saw my "RC pile." The stack of papers and books had been in a box under my bed and now was occupying a corner on my overcrowded and oversized desk.

"May I?" he asked as he pointed at the article at the top of the pile, depicting a decayed Maciel. I nodded, and as he held the article, he read: "It Has Been Confirmed - Marcial Maciel, Founder of the Legion of Christ, a Fraud!" "Catholic Order Jolted by Reports That Its Founder Led a Double Life," he continued reading.

I couldn't get used to the profound meaning and deep consequences that those statements had on people's lives... on my life. Not that Maciel's actions mattered anymore; however, the founder's pathology had been present in our day-to-day life, and it had taken me a decade to weed it out.

Edward and I stood by the desk looking down at the articles as he placed them back on the pile. Then I felt his eyes steady on me. I could tell his mind was debating: *Should I ask about it... or ignore it?* I smiled to myself, thinking it was probably a question men face in their life multiple times: *Should I give my woman the opportunity to talk? But then, if I ask, she will not stop talking.*

Noticing my smile, he smiled back and said: "I guess I shouldn't ask if this sparks joy."

We laughed.

"Very funny," I replied.

He took one of the articles again, and sat down on the bed. I sat next to him.

I reread both articles that morning. I had read them when they first came out, but I had been frazzled then, and the information did not sink in back then. It was an atrocity... criminal malevolence! I couldn't get past the explicit descriptions and the accusations... So many testimonies... and all of them coincided. Marcial had sexual intercourse with 12 year olds, 13 year olds, and sustained the "relationships" for years. He had been a serial pedophile. He had used bribes and threats to keep people quiet. The Vatican had kept silence for decades, until Maciel was an old man suffering from dementia.

"I'm sorry," Edward said as he put the article down. "How do you feel revisiting all this?"

I couldn't help but think that Edward had just gone through a different, yet similar, process when he "re-dedicated" Ava's belongings and papers.

"You more than anyone understand–" I said, without being able to finish the sentence. I had a knot in my throat.

"Is there still a feeling of guilt for introducing other women to the order?"

I nodded. "When will it go away?" I managed to ask before I began to cry.

He placed his arm around my back and held me in a tight hug. I had kept those tears for years.

"Do you want to talk about it?"

I opened up and I let Edward in. "Someone had to be in the situation we were in to understand how it works," I explained, and continued: "First, you are isolated; then you start doubting everything you believed in... you especially doubt yourself, to the point that you distrust your own judgment... and they tell you it is a triumph! Once you are stripped away from any trust in the voice of your own conscience, you are submitted to all kinds of judgments. And finally, you are fed a foreign philosophy that was said to be divine... at 19 and sustained for 18 years... Whoever has not been in that situation, has not felt the paralysis and numbness of the mind... has not experienced how the thought process can be affected."

Then, I finally shared the questions that were killing me: "Should I feel guilty? Could I have done anything differently? Am I wrong if I try to justify myself? Am I an aggressor or a victim? I do feel the need to apologize to the whole world for having been so stupid, and to be punished for leading others astray... for believing so passionately in someone who did so much harm."

"You were a girl."

"I was 19. People marry at 19... My sister married at 19."

"Those were other times."

I felt naked. The realization of how hurt my soul had been hit me yet again. Opening my heart to Edward had been difficult and humiliating... but necessary. I told him everything: about the cilice, about the shame, the times I acted against my better judgment because it was "God's Will," about my "identity disassociation," and how—finally—my identities had become one... He was now sharing his life with "all of me."

~ ~ ~ ~

"She who does not know what her heart wants searches eternally." Caroline is sitting across from me at a small table at a coffee shop. We are having coffee together... somewhere. She is wearing her hair up in a twist; her bangs sprayed up and back. Her dress is sky-blue, with puffy shoulders and buttoned up to the neck... like the ones she wore while in the polygamous sect. "I submitted myself, my will and judgment to the prophet and his wives... my older sister-wives... for too long. I know now what my heart wants and I found it..." Caroline smiles. "Do you know what you want, Elena?" I try to respond... I can't get the words to come out from my mind and to my lips. "Ah... ah..!" The effort to speak woke me up... I then said: "I want... I found it too!"

Caroline, who had escaped a Later Day Saint sect with her eight children, had been so vivid in my dream. I smiled at the acknowledgment of my *prophetic* dreams. I repeated: I found it too."

God, I thank you for life, I love you, and I need you. Thank you for healing me.

It was bright. It was strange waking up to an empty condo; my kids were with their dad. I did not like remembering the sober silence in RC's centers. I sat on the bed. "I know what I want—me: I want to be who I am: Mexican-American, sometimes smart, sometimes distracted, always imperfect, mother, teacher, advocate, in love with Edward, animal lover and mountain girl... and I found *it;* I found *me.*" I made an announcement clear and loud to myself as soon as my facial features were awake and I could articulate what my mind had wanted to shout in the dream. "Caroline, I found it too," I said.

Chapter 29

CROSS WHILE THE TIDE IS LOW

It was colder than it should have been in late June. I left my car in the garage and walked to the lobby of the Batson College Convention Center, outside of Boston. I texted Edward and learned he was only 10 minutes away. I decided to wait for him outside. I was standing on the sidewalk wearing my bellbottom jeans. Both the sun and I were beaming that morning.

Once again, the stars had aligned. It was Thursday and Edward and I were about to embark on a three-day weekend in Boston and Maine. After that, Edward would drop me off back at Batson College Convention Center—where I was leaving my car—to work for a few days in a teacher-preparation Dual Language Schools Conference. My kids were with their dad, on their weeklong summer vacation, and Edward's were with relatives and friends.

"How is my sexy professor?" He was grinning. I love Edward's typical happy and easygoing self. He parked his Honda Odyssey, put my luggage in the back seat, gave me a warm hug, and opened the passenger door for me.

"I feel like a kid going to Disney… or better. I'm so excited," I replied. His hugs always made my heart stop a little; but this time, his touch—together with the trip's anticipation—had accelerated my pulse.

"I have the tickets… And I think we have time to go to the hotel first," he said as he closed the passenger door.

I was feeling more and more comfortable with "letting the dots connect" in my life. This was important because one of the traumas I had from being in RC was that I was afraid to let life take me to undesired places. My marriage was a consequence of that—it was a decision I made with the head alone, which still was under Maciel's brainwashing spell. The summer before, Edward and I had gotten tickets to see the band U2, also in Boston and around the same date, but a few months before, we decided to resell the tickets—which we were able to do for twice the original cost, and use that money to purchase our tickets to Spain, to walk *El Camino de Compostela*. Our plan was to go, not as a couple, but as friends in search of healing from the sad events in our past lives. At the end, Edward went by himself and I went to Monterrey since my dad was gravely ill. This time, a year later, we decided to finally see U2 in Boston, and turn it into a weekend together—if at all possible. Destiny went beyond our expectations and we had been able to plan one day in Boston and two more on the coast of Maine, on Great Diamond Island.

The trip reminded me that when we live life knowing that the dots somehow will connect, we are able to open ourselves to the innumerable gifts waiting behind every door, and to the lessons every experience brings us.

"There was a boy who not only missed his mom, but missed his mom's name—because her name was not mentioned again… I was that boy." Bono, the U2 lead singer stated as prelude to one of his songs, as he recounted his own experience of losing his mom at a young age. That was one of the first lessons of our trip. Edward and I knew that talking about Ava gave his children the opportunity to keep her memory present, which is necessary for healing. He—one way or another—had done it since her passing, but Bono's statement that night gave us the opportunity to talk about ways we could help the kids heal, ways I could help him heal. Praying to Ava is not only a way to keep her memory alive; it is also a way to transform her absence into a new type of presence. And it could be a way to transform his human love for her into an angelic one, making her absence more bearable.

The next morning after the concert, we headed to Portland, Maine to catch our passenger-only ferry to Great Diamond Island. A kind ferry passenger told us, that a sand bar connects Great Diamond and Little Diamond Islands during low tide hours—somewhere between noon and dinnertime, in the summer. During the rest of the day, the only way to travel between the islands is by ferry or water taxi. The wedding we were attending was in Little Diamond, while the only hotel or inn was in Great Diamond Island, its closest island. At the inn, we learned that the ferry schedule between islands "...well... depends."

"Sorry, it depends on what?" I asked the concierge.

"We can tell you when the ferries leave Portland in that direction but not all ferries stop at every island."

"OK, so which one stops at Great Diamond?"

"Well, for sure the 11:00 am, and after that, it depends."

We later learned that ferries stop at small islands if and when they carry passengers who request to land there, and sometimes when there are enough potential passengers waiting at the port, especially if they are waving and pleading from a distance, requesting the ferry to stop.

Since the wedding was at 12:45 pm, Edward and I decided to borrow bikes from the inn—a beautifully renovated red brick building that once served as northeastern Navy defense center—and adventure across the sandbar to the neighboring Little Diamond Island, for the wedding.

The morning of the wedding, Edward came out of the bathroom smelling delicious and with a totally preppie look—navy blue blazer, khaki pants, a light salmon shirt and an orange, salmon, and blue tie... topped with a University of Connecticut (UCONN) cap. I was wearing a pastel and crème lace and sheer fabric knee-high dress, and flat sandals. We had planned our outfits as much as we could, considering we had never attended a wedding on a Maine island.

While Edward busied himself with the safe and his phone, I sat on the edge of the bed. I was feeling comfortable being with Edward alone in a hotel room. The years of therapy paid off, I thought. In RC, it was forbidden to be by ourselves, with a man, even in a public place—let alone be alone with one in a hotel room. It was incredible to think that Maciel had established and demanded the faithful fulfillment of that and every rule, while he maintained sexual relations with men and woman at every opportunity he encountered. *It definitely takes one to know one.*

"Are you OK?" Edward perceived I had traveled again to the what-happened-during-those-years tunnel.

"Yes... fine!" I got up. *"*You smell so good!"

"I taste even better!" There… was his happy humor as always.

"Oh, yeah?" I felt my grin travel across my face.

"OK, my lady, the horses are waiting." We laughed and exited through the room's patio, ready to mount our bikes in our "fancy" outfits.

We made it across the sandbar between splashes and laughter, with our shoes hanging from our neck and shoulders.

That evening, a few minutes after our return to Great Diamond Inn, where there had been a sand bar, there was an entire body of dark Atlantic Ocean. We crossed while the tide was low and I made a point to remember to do that in my everyday life. Moments where the ocean is deep and dark are moments to stay home cuddling with loved ones. The experience taught me that as I move forward in my forever-healing life, I need to cherish adventures, but also times when we can simply rest in the company of those who warm our heart.

Chapter 30

A Car wash Moment

"Morning." Edward woke up and gave me a kiss... plus a bonus hug.

I could easily get used to being with him every day, and not having to wait days before we could see each other, or be in each other's arms.

It was our last morning together, since I had to be back in Boston for an early afternoon work session. It had felt "right" to be together, isolated in those two small islands, for almost two days, with nothing else to do other than to attend the wedding and explore—the island and each other.

During those days, we not only collected good memories, we also collected small porcelain and glass pebbles that were washed daily to one of its beaches—the Glass Beach. The legend says that not far from there, Navy officials discarded the porcelain and glass dishes and glasses used during a Commander's term before a new one would take over; then new dishes and glasses were brought in to match the new Commander's taste. And that is how so many beautiful, smooth pieces of porcelain and glass washes onto shore till this day.

On our way back to Boston, I also learned that Edward "prefers" not to drive a dirty car. While parked in Portland, Maine, Edward's van was the object of dozens of seagulls' droppings. While there were droppings all over the car, a few had fallen on the windshield. After suggesting that we stop to clean the windshield, I presumed a highway gas station would be our next destination, and soon we could be on our way to my afternoon session at Batson College, in Boston. Instead, Edward changed the GPS destination and 15 minutes later, we were at a car wash.

My first reaction was to get upset, thinking about how much I wanted to arrive to my afternoon session a few minutes early, to check in to my room and freshen up. Then, I had to put on my interpretive-researcher hat as an ethnographer. I wish I could say that my loving-girlfriend hat sufficed, but it didn't. I had spent the last 10 years of my life trying to not judge with my present mind, but rather with the mind of the Elena who made every choice along the way... And now, I knew I should look at the "car wash" event with the empathy of an ethnographer—that is, I needed to interpret it (not judge it or agree/disagree with it), from Edward's perspective, looking at the intensity of his desire to wash the car, and where this fit into his needs and values. Edward could *not* drop me off in a dirty car, especially if the dirt was bird-droppings. I laughed.

"I get it," I said, and then realized the wonderful thing that had just happened. I had learned to accept "car wash moments" in Edward's life and in other peoples' lives. Those are moments where we don't judge the rationality of the choice from our present self, or present "me," but from the subject's perspective, with everything he or she is, in the moment when he or she makes the choice. Never again would I judge Elena at 19 or Elena at 38 with the mind and the eyes of the Elena of today. The interpretation of my past choices changed forever, liberating me.

"Cross while the tide is low" and "a car wash moment," I wrote that night in my journal—at home—under the title: "New Chapter. Title: Unknown." I had been writing every detail of my life since I left RC. It had started as a way to remember what I needed to bring up in therapy; after a while, it became a delicious habit.

I went to bed feeling so much love in my heart, and so I also wrote: "Love is never wasted." I believed a lie during 18 years; I repressed deep and legitimate needs... But somehow, during that time, love had found its way into my soul and expanded like a drop of fine oil. I loved God, my students, and people I worked for, and worked with. And somehow I knew it: My love had not been wasted; it was all still in my soul.

~ ~ ~ ~

    I press my notebook against my chest. I close my eyes and hand it to the woman standing in front of me. All my life, writing has been the only key to my heart. I was reserved... I felt it was safe to be extroverted only when my pen would pick up the pieces and patch them up on a paper, allowing them to make sense. I have had secret affairs with my notebooks. They were like romances that would begin with a first page and end when I would reach the last, before a second affair would begin with a blank notebook again. And now, they know about it. The inquisition is confiscating them... Worse even, burning them alive. Would they read them? Would they lock me up in a tower if I disobey? Would a tower of emotional misery suffice? Or would they burn me too at the stake? Would the burning pain inside of my chest be enough? It didn't matter; my notebooks are gone... I am only left with the pages I press against my chest. They will never listen again, will never speak, laugh, or scream. Even if it were to open its mouth, there would be no more words to share... they would be black... burned ashes... black smoke... forever. "This notebook is a source of sin and vanity, Elena," my superior says as she snatches the last notebook that I am still holding and throws it into the fire. The notebook coughs, cries, and breathes its last. Its soul quickly reincarnates as soot... but it cannot remember anymore: punishment for serving as illegitimate lover and confidant. I reach out, hoping to caress the remains. It burns...

    I woke up. What was burning was the pain in my chest.

    Strange way to recall the day I had to do away with all of my journals. They contained lines of confusion, of pain, yearning, love, and hope. I was being transferred and I was asked not to pack them. "It is a great opportunity to detach yourself from them, don't you think?" Why hadn't I said "no"? Why had I accepted it? The pain had been so deadly that, while in RC, I never wrote again... I gave the words that clamored to come out from my heart their own punishment; I left them locked inside. For 10 more years, they walked like mentally ill patients in an asylum... all scrambled up without making sense. They needed to come out and be on paper to tell me my own story; but instead, they stayed marching absentminded and confused, not knowing their meaning because there was no one to line them up in sentences anymore.

In hindsight, I understood how ridiculous it all had been... How could they censor our own writings? By doing so, were they censoring expressing our own feelings, thoughts, and judgments? Wasn't it enough for Territorial Directors to censor papers, books, and movies, and for center directors to censor all incoming and outgoing correspondence... even electronic correspondence? Anything and everything that might "tempt" the members had been forbidden: movies with healthy criticisms of the Church or with a romantic story. If, for example, the parents of a priest in a movie kissed, the scene had to be fast-forwarded. Anything that had to do with "wrong philosophies" could not be watched. Some movies were OK for the priests but not for the consecrated women in RC. "You do not have as many years of preparation and theological studies, and Legionary priests do... so you can get confused, like all those nuns with lots of graduate degrees who went liberal after Vatican II," the priest in charge of the consecrated women had explained once. It had been RC's big loss to think less of women. They would never verbalize it explicitly, but everything showed it. It was a belief Maciel had communicated subtly, and it had trickled down to all levels of male leadership. Women's emotional needs and intuition in RC had been looked down upon. This, eventually, would break down many us, even strong and competent women.

Chapter 31

BROKEN

Japanese have a tradition called Kintsugi—when a bowl is broken, it is put back together, filling the cracks with gold, creating an even more beautiful bowl. I thought about while I repaired with glue and gold paint a 20-inch tall vase that Laney—our three-year-old rescue dog—broke. When I finished putting it together, it truly looked beautiful and better than before. It became unique, and I could see why its value would increase.

We break, but never beyond repair. I am broken, and I still fill my cracks with gold—all the growth, the love and the lessons learned. I am not ashamed of my scars, of what happened to me, of having intended to live a life that broke me, not once, but twice. The life I intend to live today is a life where my cracks are gold.

~ ~ ~ ~

After a long time still, the angel finally opens its eyes and looks at me. It's standing impassive on a rock, which surfaces in the middle of a small lake. The water is still and it reflects the blue and clear sky. Its playful and elongated image is reflected on the water as well. Its large white-feathered wings are folded on its back, mimicking its hands on its front.

As the angel extends its majestic wings, an enormous wave rises. My legs give in as the wave reaches the edge of the lake. I stumble into the water. I can still breathe. I instinctively look at my body to ensure it is still me. I now know I have not turned into a fish or water nymph. There is a sense of relief. More than ever, I need to be me: the fusion I have become, and keep becoming since she is the one who will know how to live the next stage in her life.

Noticing some colored stones on the bottom of the lake, I swim towards them. They are tombstones. One reads: "Marcial Maciel 1920-2008." As I keep staring, I see Maciel's face... the same image the newspapers had included in stories about his death: a finished man, a deceitful man, inside and out. And as I stare at the residues of the man who inflicted pain beyond words, his image fades away.

I become aware of the presence of the angel next to me. He is flapping his wings rhythmically; and with one wide-range flap, he swims away... the echo of his voice stays behind for me to hear: "He is dead, Elena, and you are alive." I still wish a harsh punishment for the man... but I forgive him.

I then continue swimming towards a set of white majestic pillars arranged in half circle... embracing a plaza, an Atlantis; but it was not Greece, it was Italy...it was the Vatican. Four men, one wearing a white tunic and three wearing red, are each hugging a pillar—Church officials. I think I can recognize them and swim towards them. The men take turn corresponding to my gaze. "Even if they don't all know it, they need your forgiveness," I hear the angel say. I cannot take my eyes away from them. "They are a minority... many more made good choices," the angel says when he saw me hesitate. "They will pay," he adds. I close my eyes... my tears mix with the water. And as I open them again, the men are gone... only the columns remain, and at the center, there is a girl... a young version of myself. The angel follows me as I swim towards her. She sits on the stone floor and has a cat on her lap. It was the kitten from my dream of "that day," the one with a half-eaten ear and bald spots where the dog had torn its skin. It was the same cat that had cried on the fig tree before falling and being pinned inside the dog's jaw.

The young version of me hands me the cat. And as I hold it close to my chest, in the same way I had done before, I examine her wounds. She has scars, but she is alive and healthy. I feel happy for saving her.

"Forgive me," the girl says. *"You are angry because I did not 'escape' sooner…because I gave up my voice and I did not advocate for myself and for others during all those years."*

"I do." *I heard myself say.* I am awake.

Epilogue

Even in the summer, the weather is usually perfect at the foot of the Blue Ridge Mountains, in North Carolina. The mountains' valley breeze subjugates the heat, and the thermometer barely reaches 80. Other than during its moments of rain showers, the emerald green and sapphire blue mountain ranges reflect a friendly sun that is warm, but not scourging.

The region has everything I love: mountains, water, mild weather, and horses. The ocean and the mountains are like two lovers that put my heart in conflict. North Carolina, however, invites both to a reunion where the contact is merely contemplative from a few hundred miles away.

Today, I am near the mountainous side in the west of the state. I stretch and inhale the mountain air. I feel the breeze touch my face.

God, I thank you for life and for helping me heal. I love you and I need you.

My present is a gorgeous wooded area at the foot of the Blue Ridge Mountains. The mountains keep calling me back, and I choose to respond. That is how sneaky destiny is. It has no resemblance to fate. Fate makes you a victim; destiny turns you into a protagonist. I was the one who decided to come here as a protagonist; then, destiny took my decision and weaved it into itself; my decision plus every gift waiting here becomes my destiny. It is happening in the same way that RC was my destiny and I accept it now as such, because it was my decision to join the movement, from which followed many gifts—both bitter and sweet, which made me who I am today. I now accept the younger version of me who chose the crooked paths and unusual doors, which the current version would never have chosen. The young one did what she could, loved what she could, and spoke only the words she could. However, I am not a better version of myself because I joined RC, or because I had my children, or found Edward... but, rather, because I have learned to continue to open doors, and to be ready to use gold for the cracks.

Our cabin has a porch, which faces a river. It is almost fall and the morning sun is still enough to heat the cabin. Did I tell you I love the seasons? They remind me of how much I should enjoy each moment because each is passing and each... is the only present season I can enjoy.

Releasing a trapped sigh, I stretch every muscle in my body again. As I stare at the horizon, my eyes stop at the summit of one of the mountain ranges. How can something seem so close and yet be so far away, like every tomorrow...with almost 1500 precious minutes between now and then?

I sit down on one of the wooden rocking chairs with the computer on my lap, and become aware that my knees and legs are a bit achy... maybe from all those years kneeling for hours in prayer, or maybe from a few falls while hiking... or the *exercise*. I smiled. Prayers, falls, or making love... it has all been worth it. As I rub my knees, I also rub the scar left by the cilice; I accept both, aching knees and scars, as part of who I am now... they remind me that I have a unique present full of humility, understanding, and love.

I feel Edward's hand on my hair, and then on my shoulder. I consider "escaping"... again... but this time from the computer and from writing this book. The cabin and the man standing behind me are all I want for the moment. And so, this "black bird" who—as in the Australian Aborigines' traditions—carries stories, puts aside the computer and continues to build her destiny and live the life she intends to live.

THE END

Author's Note

The diagnosis I give the Legion and Regnum Christi's Founder, Fr. Marcial Maciel, in this book, is that of an abusive narcissist. His life, as a ghost protagonist, intertwines with my life mainly through the chronicle of short scenes.

Maciel influenced the movement's members tremendously, hunting some of us even after his death. Marie-France Hirigoyen, in her book *Stalking the Soul*, a systematic collection of cases of narcissism, describes how narcissists tend to build bonds with others, practically sucking their sense of security and ego and disarming them first in order to convince them later that the roles have reversed—the abusive one becomes the victim, and the narcissist's victim becomes the abuser. As a consequence, the true victims remain paralyzed. The narcissist's presence becomes the dazzling headlights of a hunting jeep, blinding the prey to the point that it remains silent and subdued, becoming the narcissist's accomplice. Typically, abusive narcissists are intelligent individuals who, at a young age, suffer with such intensity that—to survive—they create their own reality: their own world, with their own rules where they are the megalomaniac authority. A clear parallelism with "religious" perverts—such as Brian David Mitchell (Elizabeth Ann Smart's captor), or Carolyn Jessop's polygamous abusive husband Merril Jessop (former FLDS member)—is abundantly clear as presented in the victims' memoirs, which I highly recommend. The perverse minds of their aggressors used religion to satisfy their twisted egos in the same way Maciel did.

Maciel's pathology, his obsessive need for triumph, and his autocratic personality led him to create "his immortal legacy" without measuring the cost.

In addition to this diagnosis and traits, others have been attributed. I chose these since I considered them to be, from my viewpoint, the ones that affected the life of RC members the most.

VIGNETTES FROM RESEARCH AND THE IMAGINATION

The following vignettes are not part of my memoir. They are the fruit of some research and my imagination. They offered the mind stories on how and why Maciel committed and justified his crimes. I changed the names, places and dates in the stories to protect the identity of the victims, and because I combined reality with fiction.

Maciel's Punishment, 1956

Maciel had to go against his will. Because of his temporary suspension as the Legion's Director, he was still not allowed to have "contact" with his seminarians. He was punished, and so he had to do with Anna Lopez. He was inviting the never-forgotten mermaid to spend a few days with him in Majorca. Maciel enjoyed traveling in Spain when Brother Ruben could not accompany him. Ruben spoke several languages. Maciel could only speak Spanish. As a young boy, he had tried to learn English but, unable to stand the way people made fun of him when he couldn't get the accent perfect, he stopped trying altogether. Later on, when someone would ask if he could speak another language—since many Legion members could—Maciel would state that he had been the grain buried underground so others could become tall stalks of wheat. He would typically then clarify that due to the demands of his schedule—his studies, the classes he had to teach, the time he had to dedicate to spiritual guidance and confessions, plus the innumerable trips to raise money—there had been no time to expand his studies. In fact, Maciel had been ordained a priest at 24, barely finishing his theological studies. He had been on the fast track. He saw the need to clarify because rumor had it that he never finished his studies and had paid his way to ordination.

The car stopped on the street outside the restaurant and hotel where Anna and Maciel had spent an evening together... followed by a night heated by the Andalusia autumn humidity and pleasure. He was wearing civilian clothes... white and khaki as usual. He felt handsome with his blond hair slicked back, and his fashionable gold-rimmed eyeglasses. He made reservations at the Perl, one of the most prestigious passenger boats traveling from Cadiz to Majorca. He would be embarking that evening. His budget was generous... no doubt he and the girl would have a good time. He had introduced himself to the captain early that day. The man had seemed pleased to know Marcial was traveling with his alleged niece, daughter of the sister who had presumably married Don Lopez, the Andalusian; all of them, fictitious characters formulated in the Marcial's realistic story. The trip would be a platform Maciel would use in order to learn how wealthy Spaniards went about life. He had been successful in Mexico. He had raised enough funds to subsist adequately. He was paying for his trip with the latest donation, the inheritance of an old woman.

The explanation was simple. His brother-in-law, Don Rodrigo Lopez, had asked him to take Anna away a few days in the name of Christian charity, since the daughter seemed to be an untamable young mare. In reality, Maciel did not know who Anna's parents were, or how worried they were about her untamable state... but that could explain his niece's potentially obscene behavior on the boat. Also, their rooms would be next to each other to ensure he could keep an eye on the girl. To Anna, the trip would be presented as an opportunity to travel... the trip in exchange for her "services." Anna would not resist the offer.

"Good day!" Maciel greeted as he entered the restaurant.

"G' day" replied the man behind the bar. Three men who had previously been talking at a nearby table turned to observe the man who had spoken with a distinctive accent. "Would you like a table?" the bartender added.

As soon as the three men continued their conversation, Maciel came close to the man and discreetly handed him a wad of bills. "I am looking for my niece, Anna Maria Lopez. Do you know where I can find her?" Uncles typically knew their nieces' and nephews' middle names... Anna Maria sounded right.

The bartender took the money casually and placed it in his apron pocket together with the rest of the day's tips. He remembered Maciel... and he remembered the girl who had kept the man company some months back.

"Anna..." he said with a smile, but looking at the counter as he cleaned it with a rag. "You will find her at the Gran Plaza Hotel. She cleans rooms there," the man continued without looking back at Maciel. He then moved on to serve a Porto one of the men had requested.

So Anna was making a living decently, Marcial thought... Maybe that was to his advantage. The girl had potential. He had a good eye for people.

On his way to the hotel, Maciel stopped to buy some cigars for the trip, courtesy of the widow... or Don Lopez, Anna's father... Marcial repeated it as if by doing so, it would become true.

The Gran Plaza was a delight to the eye. Its majestic murals, columns, and towers echoed Andalusia's beauty. It possessed Spaniard strength, and the curves and colors the Muslim architecture brought to the region during their invasion prior to Queen Isabella and Ferdinand II. The people in the lobby were equally elegant and beautiful. He imagined Anna... wild Anna trying to fit in among them.

"Good afternoon. May I help you?" a man asked behind the concierge's desk as Maciel approached.

"Good afternoon. I am looking for my niece Anna Maria Lopez," replied Marcial with a warm smile, looking straight into the man's eyes.

"Anna just began her shift, Mister..."

"Rivero, Pascal Rivero. Could you please tell her that I am here... and that her persistence... wanting to work her way up starting as maid, is becoming very annoying. We are boarding the Perl tonight and have no time to waste." Besides the girl's last name and her body, Maciel remembered that when Anna had tried to get information out of him, he had successfully turned the questions around and had found out she came from a small town in the region, and that she had been in Cadiz for only two months... Most likely, the concierge would not question the kinship. "I will wait outside." Maciel's face was expressionless and matter of fact as he walked out, stopping at the porch.

Anna showed up a few minutes later wearing trendy sneakers, and a pair of slim pants closing right above her ankles... they were light yellow. Her button-down, sleeveless white blouse was made of a fine cotton... the best way to ventilate the heat that prematurely arrived to the southern cost every year. She approached Maciel, rocking her hips slowly and looking down into her purse. She took out a cigarette and looking at "Pascal," smiled. Her skin was not as tan as it had been in the fall. She had grown up. She showed it by the way she gazed at the young and handsome man who had returned looking for her, for what she could "produce."

"Hello, Don Pascal, my dear uncle. It is so nice to see you." She was still wearing a smile on both, lips and eyes... framed by beautiful short curls… Only they had remained golden.

Maciel returned the smile and leaned down to kiss her... a kiss on each cheek as customary in the region. "I came with a proposal." Anna could appreciate his youthful and attractive look at 38. "Tonight I leave for Palma de Majorca. We will travel on a luxurious boat for a couple of days, and stay for a week at one of the best hotels in Palma. I would like you to come with me."

Anna kept her eyes on the ground, on some pebbles she was tossing around with the tips of her flats, while holding a smile and keeping her hands on the hips. "How do you make your money, Uncle Pascal? I am trying to figure out why the uncle-niece relationship is more convenient than that of cousins."

"I work for the CIA, and the job does not give me the opportunity to foster relationships. Nevertheless," he gave her a smile reserved for women when he was not playing the role of priest, "I have some days off and I would like to have a darn good time... with a generous budget." Maciel emphasized the word "generous." "Enough for a complete wardrobe and gifts... or the equivalent in money, it's up to you, if you will be smart enough to take advantage of the opportunity."

After a pause, Anna said: "Very well... so I'm your niece. Or what am I exactly, Pascal?"

Maciel explained the plan, overdoing the formality, as if it were one of his many work plans he had to present at a meeting, as a CIA agent.

They agreed she would call him uncle Marcial, since that was his first name, and not Pascal. He explained to Anna that it was all right for passengers to know his fake identity as priest: Marcial Maciel, Legionary of Christ... it was part of a master plan. He omitted telling her that he would win over passengers to gain their trust and ask them for generous donations.

During the trip, both shared their goods. Maciel was generous with his money, sense of humor, warm smile, and advice. He was very entertaining during conversations with crew and passengers, winning everyone's admiration and even affection. He had already studied the list of passengers so he knew who was worth "cultivating" and who would be a waste of time. Anna, on the other hand, shared with Maciel her body and her lovemaking techniques, as well as much laughter and good humor. The girl seemed to be in outstanding shape and used every body muscle with a purpose. Maciel appreciated her flexibility of character and body in addition to the opportunity to challenge his physique.

By the end of the trip, Anna had a complete wardrobe, and a beautiful pearl necklace and bracelet. She also had enough cash for six months' rent and a job as waitress at the Grand Plaza Hotel. Considering the girl's knockout smile and ways, she would make as much in tips as in salary. One of the hotel's owners had been onboard the Pearl on their way back. Maciel had won over the favor from him.

The following year in the spring, when Maciel visited Cadiz, he found out Anna was living now in Seville, happily married to the son of a successful international company owner. Maybe the wardrobe, pearls, and Maciel's advice had been a good investment after all. He was pleased. He did not need her anymore... The Vatican had concluded the investigation and found him a worthy priest and general director. He had been reintegrated to the community as a hero for enduring calumnies, and was enjoying plenty of "contact" with the seminarians, just like before. He definitively preferred them over Anna, or any other woman, for that matter.

Maciel and a Second Woman, 1976

The taxi arrived to a tall bronze gate built to mimic a bamboo wall. A middle-aged man with dark skin approached the car. The man in the back seat identified himself: "It's Father Maciel, Raul. I came to visit Mr. Paco for a few days."

"Ah... yes! Father Maciel, of course... I almost did not recognize you... come on in!" The doorman kept his hand over his wrinkled dark eyes to prevent the late afternoon ocean-bay sun from blinding him.

The priest was wearing khaki pants and a white button down shirt with rolled-up sleeves. He was 56 but his appearance was still young. He had started to color his hair dark blond years back. No one in the Legion questioned it. Of course, others outside the Legion had raised eyebrows. Maciel had explained that one morning, after the enemies conspiring against him had attacked with false accusations, he woke up to find that his entire head had gone gray... It had already happened to a saint in the Church... or had it been Marie Antoinette, before she was decapitated? Either way, it was unwise to let the enemy think they had gained control over him... and so, Maciel dyed his hair, and had done it ever since. It was all for the Kingdom; for the sake of Christ's Kingdom, the world needed to see him strong.

As the gate opened, the car traveled through a driveway, descending towards the only home on the property. The palm trees by the side of the windy road seemed to bow to greet him. The beautiful mansion had been built in the 1950s and it reflected the organic architecture and the overuse of glass, typical of the period. It was a copy of one of Lloyd Wright's works, Paco Marquez used to boast. The fresh white paint covering the gigantic boxes with abundant walls of glass confessed to have witnessed years of scarlet sunsets, children playing, women in the latest swimming-wear fashion, and men enjoying a cigar and a drink while securing a business deal or cursing at the thought of a corrupt Mexican politician. This was Maciel's world just as much as the altar where he celebrated Mass on festivities, the bed where he had sex with his "chosen ones," and the gatherings with Vatican officials.

Raul, who had run down the path and was now carrying the priest's luggage, led him into the house. A very young woman with a rounded face and dark brown hair, almost as brown as her eyes, welcomed him. "I will let Don Paco know that you are here. What can I offer you to drink?"

"Thanks... a whiskey, please. What's your name?"

"Sarah."

"Have we met before?"

"I don't think so. Please excuse me." The girl seemed in a hurry to leave. As the woman disappeared through one of the doors, Maciel thought of Anna... and another young woman he had met in Miami. He could not recall her name. Sarah seemed helpless as well... young... very young. Where had he seen her?

Maciel approached the terrace, a continuation of the elegant and vast living room at the center of the house. The water of the bay was melting the sun like it did every evening. The only sound was that of a mocking bird and the melodious water fountains tactfully distributed throughout the garden. Maciel could smell the salt of the breeze mixed with *ceviche* and gin.

"Impressive, isn't it?" Don Paco's hoarse and jolly voice came from the pool cabana. He walked around the pool away from the rail separating the property from the cliff.

"Very! How are you Don Paco?" Maciel knew the successful young businessman enjoyed being referred to with formality.

"Not as blond as you, my dear priest! Look at me..." He pointed at his voluminous black and white hair. "On the other hand you--"

"—I am at disadvantage, Don Paco." Maciel interrupted. "It is good to see you and thanks for receiving me. I have to write some documents and your divine place can inspire a donkey." Maciel offered a grin.

Sarah joined them and handed Maciel a glass with ice and a golden drink. "Thanks."

"Maciel, this is Sarah. She is staying here for a few weeks."

"Yes, we met... Sarah, I have a feeling we have met before," the priest insisted.

"Excuse me." The girl was gone in no time without replying.

"She is shy... Her father used to work for me. Both her mom and dad passed away last month in a terrible car accident. I offered a place to stay until she figures out what she wants to do. I believe she is a waitress in one of the restaurants in town—"

"—Ah! Maybe that's why her face seems so familiar."

Maciel had been at the restaurant where Sarah worked several nights a week. And so he went back... and back again... and again.

Once Maciel explained to Sarah that he was a CIA agent and that was why he had the money to help her with her plans, Sarah became "close" to him. And they both settled in an apartment in Rome, Italy... part time, of course.

Maciel and a Third Woman, 1978

MACIEL: I have to get up... I need to get dressed before someone finds me. I am hurting. Was that blood on the hay? Why did the other two have to show up? Why wouldn't James kick their arse? I tried... Now my chest and my face hurt too. Mama will worry. How can I take it away? Where can I clean? How can I cover up before Mama sees me? Oh, Mama, please don't see me and don't tell Papa. I am OK. I am a man, you see? I can protect myself. Oh, Mama, don't cry.

~ ~ ~ ~

Maciel woke up and could not get back to sleep. It was afternoon anyhow, and he needed to get up. Some fresh air and a walk on the beach would surely help him feel better. His mother had died the year before. He was feeling lonely in that hotel room. He had written about it in a letter he drafted that morning. At the end, he threw the letter away because it had many grammatical errors and it was too simple. It was not like the rest of the correspondence his secretaries helped him draft. "You had something I had to sacrifice..." Maciel used to tell these young man appointed to serve him as secretaries, "You had those writing classes at the seminary. So please embellish the letters I am dictating."

Some days ago, he had found out his enemies were hitting hard. The Pope, Paul VI, had died and the Prefect of the Congregation of Religious had attempted to open his case. Would he find the files he had paid to secure after the 1950s accusations? The word was: there were new accusations against him and, presumably, there were new proofs of his addiction and his homosexual "relationships," including the sexual abuses of minors. Some of them involved fraud and the misuse of money. Others were old accusations that had surfaced. Fabio and Peter were plotting against him. Even Ruben had broken his word, and had joined the other two presenting accusations and alleged proofs. When Ruben left the Legion, some months back, he had been warned about the fact that though Maciel wouldn't hurt him—an irony since he had hurt him pretty badly all right— his friends could still hurt him. So he ought to keep quiet. Fabio did not let himself be intimidated and now, he and his colleagues in virtue and crime—literally—were preparing a case against Maciel. Maciel felt tired and betrayed. He had put in place some mechanisms to defend himself... lobbying with key people in the Church. It should work... everything would be OK. The accusations were not likely to go beyond Mexico's Church authorities and the nunciature. And since, supposedly, some of the "incidents" had occurred in Ireland, Italy, and Spain, he had made arrangements with Church authorities in those countries as well. Nevertheless, Ireland's nuncio was stubborn and might have already gone to the Vatican with the gossip. Fabian and Ruben would go straight to the Vatican as well... but they would hardly accomplish anything there. It was the word and hurt ego of two men who had been contradicted and humiliated. They had expected to be given an important job... instead, they had been asked to serve humbly as subjects in the missions or at a school, and their ego had not been able to tolerate it... Their resentment had led them to make up lies against Maciel. That is the explanation the founder had offered with an air of holiness and wisdom... He had expressed his own hurt and confusion at the accusations. "It is hard to believe that human pride and greed can reach such extremes and crazy behavior... to the point of making up calumnies. They want to finish me, Your Eminence," Maciel had clarified.

Maciel was now walking on the beach by the water. He was wearing a button-down cotton shirt and trousers he had folded up to prevent the salty water from ruining them. The Pacific Ocean was beautiful. Even the whales were celebrating its beauty, flying in and out of the water... They could be seen at a distance. It was a marvelous show. They will go away to rest soon, together with the sun. What about him? Would he go to rest as well? Could he rest? He could go back to the hotel where he had rented a room... Thank God, most places in southern California had bilingual staff.

As he passed some rocks, the beach continued and he saw a toddler. He was building a sand tower and ran to show his mother something he had found in the sand; probably a pebble smoothed by the underwater dances that lasted millions of years. The woman turned to him and smiled when she heard him calling her. She had been looking at Maciel. She was young, not even 20; Maciel, on the other hand, was 58. Marcial approached the woman who was sitting under an umbrella. She was busy putting away the leftovers of what could have been the child's snack... maybe her snack as well: grapes, Ritz crackers, and something in a thermos. She wore a purple one-piece bathing suit. When she realized a man was approaching her, she put on a white top and as she buttoned it, she heard the greeting: "Good afternoon." His voice was relaxed and low. "I heard the child calling you in Spanish. I was relieved since I do not speak English well. I can see you are about to leave, could you kindly help me with something?"

Sonia would have never accepted to speak to a stranger at that time of the day... and on the beach. She had a little boy with her and the place was deserted. But the man was different. He seemed sophisticated. His clothes and glasses seemed expensive. He looked trustworthy, his smile was warm and there was kindness in his eyes. He had to be someone well educated and honest.

"What can I do for you, sir?"

First Daughter, 1981

"I like the way that dress looks... I'll get you some more while we are here. Spanish fabric is better than the fabric in Mexico or the States... by far." The couple had hugged discreetly and gotten into a taxi at the airport in Majorca.

"It is showing now, you know." Sarah rested a hand on her stomach.

"Yes... I can see. How are you feeling?"

"Great, thanks."

Maciel had made a reservation at the same hotel where he had stayed with Anna almost 30 years before... He had requested the same room. He could look forward to a night of relaxation and pleasure. But he needed to find the way to bring "it" up without scaring her... especially now that she would give him a child.

He requested room service... They need to keep themselves in the privacy of their room. It was 1986 and by now, his picture had been in Spain's ABC several times, and he could not afford to be recognized... Those Spaniards were astute.

"Sarah, are you seeing a doctor?"

"What do you mean, a gynecologist... why? Yes, I already went to my first visit as you suggested last time we spoke." Sarah had unpacked and taken a shower, washed her hair and brushed her teeth... This time, she didn't forget to use floss. Her mouth smelled exactly the way he liked it. She was now sitting on the bed, combing her long black hair wearing a white and long silk nightgown with its matching robe. She had never again worn a negligee... the last time she did, he told her she looked cheap... "Someone from your origins has to wear the clothing of a lady... otherwise you look... cheap." The "cheap" said with a frown. She had whispered coyly that it was silk and that the lady at the store had assured her it was the latest... It was a red lace one-piece thong and push-up bra. "It was one of those expensive stores for ladies like the ones you show me in the magazines... where Don Paco and his wife appear." To which Maciel had responded with an air of superiority, "If you want to wear those things that make you look low-class, wear them with someone else... They might even slip you a bill or two."

"So, did the doctor say everything was alright?"
"Yes... why?"
"The baby is healthy?"
"Well... yes, he said everything was normal. Why?"
"And you? Did he examine you in that area?"
"Yes... he had to... I hope you don't mind."
"And what did he say?"
"Well, that I am fine, of course." Sarah put the comb on the night table and she leaned back on the pile of pillows waiting for the couple.
"Well... that's good. You have kept your promise, right?"
"Of course!" She patted next to her on the bed with a reassuring smile... the smile that he wouldn't criticize...the one that was seductive enough but sophisticated, shy, and warm at the same time.

Maciel corresponded and positioned himself on his stomach. Sarah began with the back massage... She straddled him with a leg on each side. The priest, pseudo CIA agent, relaxed under her girlish... rounded figure. "It is good you are healthy." He seemed in a daze.

It was indeed good... If she was healthy, he was healthy too. Father Reyes had not been as lucky. The good old priest, superior of one of his communities, had been crying on the phone the week before. He had come down with herpes. "How can it be *Nuestro Padre*... why?" Maciel had remained silent and heard the man for a few minutes. *Really, Father?* he had thought... and then added in his head without saying it: *Did you really think the body of a priest would be exempt from sexually transmitted diseases? Did he really think God would spare him from getting whatever dirty disease the whore he "used" every Sunday* carried? *What was he thinking?* "Father, maybe God is trying to tell you something... Maybe abstinence is a better idea for you," Maciel had remarked on the phone.

Some years back, Father Reyes had decided to leave the Legion because he wanted... he "needed"... to be with a woman. He had not added, like most Legion priest who found chastity too difficult, that he was lonely and wanted companionship. His was a simple case of testosterone-fueled sex drive. Maciel had implicitly given him permission to visit a decent brothel on a regular basis, with the condition that he made arrangements so no one who knew him as a priest would find out. It had started with Maciel giving him the address of a benefactor he had to visit on Sunday afternoons... he had requested it in front of the entire community. When Father Reyes had arrived to the address Father Maciel had provided, the number did not exist. It was outside of the city and there was not much around... But not too far from where the nonexistent street number was supposed to be, there was a modest home... A woman was sipping cold tea, sitting on the porch. "I was waiting for you," she had said. She was an attractive woman in her 30s... maybe 40. As Reyes approached the house's porch, she got up and opened the front door, walked in, and waited for him in the foyer. For a benefactor, she surely had a modest home, the priest had thought... Then, at a closer look, he saw that she was wearing a zip-down leather dress that would have to be peeled off. To the man's expectant surprise, she had taken his hand and had walked him into one of the rooms with dimmed lights and a large bed in the center. The rest had become a blur. A woman with almost no clothes was waiting for him by the bed... like a spider waits by the web.

For six years, since that day, Reyes, had "religiously" visited the benefactor, just as Maciel had asked... Did he ask, or suggest... or was it a trick played on him by destiny? Had he been on the wrong street?

That will teach the horny bastard a lesson, Maciel thought before he closed his eyes again. Sarah was now straddling him as he lay facing up. He did not have to worry about all that... Sarah and the others had different habits... And he... just like Reyes, had gotten what he deserved: followers, faithful subjects, lovers and children... a son, and maybe a daughter. He also had money. For 20 years he had been putting money aside in the Cayman Islands and in Switzerland. His strategy was perfect... *Catch me if you can.*

From the Mouths of Babes, Drunks, and Drug Addicts, 1988

His troublesome enemies would not leave him alone. That afternoon, Mexico's nuncio called Maciel to give him a heads-up. It was 1988 and additional accusations had arrived to the *nunciature*... copies of documents. The originals had gone straight to the Prefect of the Congregation of the Faith in the Vatican, Cardinal Ratzinger.

"Congregation of the Faith… but why?" Maciel had not been the same since his brain stroke the previous year, which followed a series of complications.

"As you know," the Nuncio explained calmly, "the Pope just delegated to the Congregation of the Faith the handling of accusations of that sort... of sexual abuse." The nuncio was aware of Maciel's delicate physical state and was choosing his words carefully.

Indeed, according to *Pastor Bonus,* the Apostolic Constitution on the Roman Curia, promulgated by Pope John Paul II on June 28, 1988, "The proper duty of the Congregation for the Doctrine of the Faith is to promote and safeguard the doctrine on faith and morals in the whole Catholic world; so it has competence in things that touch this matter in any way." The Pontiff had included in the "package" all investigations of *delicta graviora* accusations... crimes which the Church considered extremely serious: those against the Eucharist, abuse of the sacrament of Confession, and anything that had to do with the sixth commandment: "Thou shall not commit adultery"... especially crimes committed by clergy against minors. The Congregation of the Faith, and its Prefect—Cardinal Ratzinger—were made the "promoters of justice" who dealt, among other things, with priests accused of pedophilia.

"Who is the Prefect?" Maciel's voice reflected frustration. He was supposed to know but was having a hard time remembering… His head was pounding… probably needed one more pill.

"Ratzinger... Cardinal Joseph Aloisius Ratzinger, the German Cardinal."

...*Damn!* Ratzinger was known to be straight as an arrow. Maciel knew he would accept no bribe. But he was prudent and thorough... and he loved the Pope... and the Pope loved Maciel. The Legion had been growing. They had just opened a seminary in Brazil; the ones in Spain, Ireland, Mexico, and the United States were overflowing with new vocations. There were members in almost 30 countries... and their student body and monetary worth had quadrupled within 10 years... They had tens of thousands of students and millions—or was it billions—of dollars. The Church would try to declare him innocent... that was what they did. Or at least, that was what they had done until then. Would things change with Ratzinger? It was different before... when he was small, his work was small. Now... too much was at risk. The Legion was the Church and if there was a scandal in the Legion, it would be a Church scandal. Besides, it did not all depend on Ratzinger. Even if he were to decide to open the investigation, which knowing him, he probably would, Serrano—the Vatican's Secretary of State—would not allow it. Serrano was not only Maciel's friend; the two men also "helped" each other. Maciel cared for almost every single need Serrano had.

The accusations were incredible... Nevertheless, one of the witnesses had been a priest from a diocese in California who, on his deathbed, after 20 years of exemplary priesthood, had signed–in the presence of his bishop–a statement swearing that everything he had said regarding Maciel's sexual and emotional abuses was true. The bishop had been so deeply touched by the testimony of the dying man that he had traveled to Rome to deliver the deceased man's testimony by hand, to the Prefect of the Congregation of the Faith. He had attached to it his own letter witnessing the priest's last 20 years of life, and the way he died... leaving it to God to do justice.

"This poor old priest was mentally ill, some genetic tendency that we detected late in the Legion," Maciel told the nuncio... "Out of Christian charity, we kept him in the community and cared for him until he lost it completely and said he wanted to go. Apparently, he fabricated his own asylum next to a man who holds a grudge against the Legion..." Maciel said, referring to the bishop. "Wasn't he a Jesuit?" he added, as if the mention of the rival order would explain the animosity. "I even have a report from a psychiatrist that explains his pathology. I could probably send you a copy if you wish. The psychiatrist explained he tends... well, he tended... to make things up and confuse the facts. He believed his stories to the point that he became credible to those who were unaware of his condition. That could explain the bishop's reaction when the man died." Maciel moaned, "May God keep him in his mercy!"

Maciel was exhausted. "Ungrateful traitors!" he exclaimed once he had hung up the phone. He looked through the window. The garden extended to the next block and was beautifully kept by a gardener. He was staying at one of the five houses the Legion owned in Mexico City... all of them crowded. Everything would be OK. They were powerful. He was powerful.

Someone knocked at the door. A man, rather rounded, with fair skin, rosy cheeks, and small blue eyes peeked through the door.

"Father Damien, please come in. Can you get me my pills... and a brandy?" Maciel let his body sink into his leather chair at the desk.

"*Nuestro Padre*, you just took a couple."

"I need to sleep." Damien asked no more questions... He reached for the bottle he had kept in one of the cabinets and poured the brandy. As soon as he placed the pills on the desk, Maciel took them and popped both into his mouth, swallowing them with a sip of brandy. "Do you have any new jokes, Father Damien?"

Damien was from England and took great pleasure in keeping Fr. Maciel amused. "I do, *Nuestro Padre.*" The priest stopped to think... he was still standing by the desk. "How does one call a Kerry man under a wheelbarrow?" Damien asked promptly. He had been born next to county Kerry and the rivalry motivated the Irish priest to remember most of those jokes.

"Let's see... What do you call a Kerry man under a wheelbarrow?" Maciel looked at Damien expectantly... a smile already on his face.

"A mechanic!" They laughed. Then Maciel got up and went to lie down. Conveniently, his room was both bedroom and office, furnished with a bed and a desk, his chair, and two additional chairs on the opposite side.

Damien needed to speak to Maciel about some pressing matters... but his founder had just fallen asleep... or that is what it seemed. He let his heavyset body descend slowly on one of the two smaller leather chairs opposite the desk, and leaned his head back... He closed his eyes. Maciel was like a father to him... but what a nightmare it had become to control his mood swings in front of third parties who wouldn't understand... They would judge his beloved founder.

He needed to get *Nuestro Padre* to rest... to get better... and not worse, not back to the hospital. The weeks Maciel had spent at hospitals after the hemorrhagic stroke he suffered—first in Mexico City and then in Houston—had not gone well. The founder had been out of control... and they had spent a fortune, keeping people out of his business. The nurses had tried to save everything used by Maciel... even bandages, saying he would be a canonized saint since he was a founder in the Church, like Saint Francis, who founded the Franciscans; until Maciel woke up from the coma, and began to talk.

"Doctor, tell this ugly nurse to go brush her teeth, her breath stinks." Maciel's dry lips had muttered the harsh statement as he was slowly recovering consciousness.

"What?" the woman who had been checking his vitals said indignantly. Dr. Guerra signaled the woman to leave.

"I want you to replace her. I need someone who is better prepared and clean," Maciel told the doctor.

"Of course, Father Maciel."

"You should see how I train my women," Maciel continued sleepy but animated. "I do a marvelous job. I make them understand that when heaven does not favor their looks, they cannot lose points smelling bad. Anyone with minimum intelligence would know that."

The doctor continued taking notes, and then said, "Well, your women are very lucky to have you, Father. What are their names?" He needed to know if his memory had been affected.

"Sarah," Maciel said. "I actually need to call her. She just had a daughter, you know... my daughter. She looks just like me... though she got her mama's eyes."

"I didn't know you had a daughter, Father. Where do they live?" The doctor needed to have someone corroborate the information.

"Yes... Not many people know. We met in Mazatlan." After a pause, the priest continued, "Well, the one I don't want to speak to right now is Sonia... she is a vampire." The doctor released a chuckle. "You know... a vampire... She sucks and sucks... and not precisely where we men like it." Dr. Guerra saw what he thought were the dreamy eyes of an experienced man. He was confused now. "It is the sucking that steals your life... time, money. Ah! But she gave me a son, my firstborn—" Father Damien stormed into the room... "Ah! Damien, tell the doctor about my son..."

"You have many sons, *Nuestro Padre*... Sons and daughters in spirit—I can see he is tired, doctor. Shouldn't he be resting? How long has he been awake?" There was irritation and worry in his voice... his red eyes were surrounded by dark circles.

"About half an hour ago... Yes, he might need to rest. His vitals are good and his faculties seem normal... Father Maciel," Dr. Guerra measured his words carefully, "you are aware of the recent studies linking morphine to certain types of strokes, aren't you?"

"No...why?"

"Well, morphine is a vasodilator, and its use over prolonged periods widens all the blood vessels. If the person suffers a small hemorrhage in the brain, or even a diminutive leak, the morphine effects would widen the blood vessel, expanding the leak... and if the blood pressure is high enough, there will be more blood flow and therefore, a stroke. I would suggest you stop using it."

"Oh... Fr. Maciel just uses it in small doses, when the doctor prescribes it," Father Damien explains.

"Well... that's not what the exams show, Father. The facts don't lie."

Riding my favorite horse, Colorado, at my grandfather's working ranch, Tamaulipas, Mexico.

With Fr. Marcial Maciel LC, during his visit to the Regnum Christi center in Rhode Island, fall of 1990.

Made in the USA
Middletown, DE
16 September 2020

19881372R00144